ARAB SOCIALISM

by
ABDEL MOGHNY SAID

with a Section by
M. SAMIR AHMED

D1072798

BARNES & NOBLE BOOKS · NEW YORK
(a division of Harper & Row Publishers, Inc.)

© Blandford Press Ltd. 1972
Published In The U.S.A. 1972 by
HARPER & ROW PUBLISHERS, INC.
BARNES & NOBLE IMPORT DIVISION.

ISBN 06 4960692

Printed in Great Britain by
Northumberland Press Limited
Gateshead

ARAB SOCIALISM

CONTENTS

Introduction

Stretching across the world from the River Euphrates to the Atlantic Ocean lie the sunny but troubled Arab lands. Historically this has been an area whence some of humanity's most significant ideas have originated and where the current of human forces has often been strong and their clash explosive.

The three great monotheistic religions sprang from the Arabian homeland and vital elements of the ancient civilisations were brought to Europe by the Arabs in the seventh, eighth and ninth centuries. In more recent times, the Suez Canal, Middle East oil and the battlefields of the Western Desert are associated with the growth and survival of the Europe we know today.

Here is the bridge-land between Asia, Africa and Europe; as it is between the industrialised north and the southern hemisphere with its largely rural economy. It is here too that the technically proficient world of the 'haves', as represented by Israel, has thrust itself precipitately into the arms of the developing world. Here focuses perhaps the greatest challenge to modern man; that of pioneering a radically new relationship whereby the minority world of the rich West may become acceptable to the vast developing territories of the rest of the world. On its ability to achieve this transformation may well hang the world's capacity to survive in freedom.

In this perspective, it is clearly important for the Wes-

1

tern world to become far more adequately informed about the issues of the Middle East, and this presentation of Arab Socialism is offered as a contribution towards this end. But before embarking on the main subject certain background facts should be recalled.

The Middle East, with the United States and Russia sponsoring opposing sides in the Israeli-Arab confrontation, is in the view of President Nixon, the area most likely to trigger off a third world war. In addition to this, it supplies some eighty-five per cent of Europe's essential oil needs and therefore it is a direction from which could come, should the oil flow ever be suspended, a major threat to the European economy.

For many years the West prospected for the oil of the Middle East, extracted it, paid a royalty on it, shipped it, refined it and marketed it. Meanwhile in most of the producer countries their share of the oil wealth was finding its way to a limited ruling circle whose interests coincided with those of the oil companies. This is not to deny that oil revenues were directed in many instances into enlightened channels such as free education and medical services as in Saudi Arabia and Kuwait; but the oil interests of the 'have' nations of the West coincided broadly with those of the 'have' minority in the countries of origin.

Now, however, a new situation has arisen, as events in Libya have illustrated. King Idris, in his late seventies, was persuaded that his country needed a sophisticated Western defence system with ground-to-air missiles of the sort supplied to NATO. Conscious of the tendency of armies to take over the reins of government as in the case of neighbouring Egypt and Algeria, Idris saw the missiles as a way of defending his country without putting the temptation of more practical weapons into the hands of his army. The cost of the deal was around two hundred and fifty million pounds sterling. Diplomats and businessmen congratulated each other, blissfully oblivious of the violent reactions this ill-fated contract would soon arouse in the army and among the nationalist minded youth of Libya.

Suddenly, on the night of 1 September 1969, a group of young officers headed by twenty-seven-year-old Lieutenant Gadhafi, took over the Army Command and forced the chief of the Armed Police to surrender. Within days the new military régime was recognised by Britain and other governments and, of course, the rocket deal was off.

The European and American oil companies now found themselves dealing with a very different type of supplier. Within a year the new Libyan régime had sent the Americans and British packing from their bases at Wheelus Field and El Adem, had expelled the remnant of the Italian colony in Tripoli and wiped out every notice and sign in the country not written in Arabic. War was declared upon 'poverty, ignorance and backwardness', and, despite wholesale dislocation resulting from these sweeping changes, a programme of 'agricultural and industrial revolution' was embarked upon. President Gadhafi proclaimed a new order of 'Islamic Arab Socialism—an Arab application of socialism'.

The negotiations in the early part of 1971 with the Libyans made it clear that the united front of the oil companies had in fact been breached and the whole price structure of Europe's most vital import was now exposed to increasingly tough bargaining by the producer countries. Almost overnight the oilmen lost their unquestioned position of strength. Control of the world's distributing machinery had been their ace card but it had now been trumped by the militancy of the Arab socialists for whom commercial arguments were not the prime consideration. In their demands for higher prices the Libyan leaders had the support of the other Arab oil-producing countries, for all resented the fact that, for example, every 35p gallon of

3

petrol in affluent Britain provided 20½p in tax to her government's coffers, 13¼p to the companies for refining and distribution, while only 1¼p went to the country which produced the oil.

Clearly both Western governments and the oil companies urgently needed to find a new understanding with the Arab Left. Former commercial laws of supply and demand were breaking down under the impact of today's ideological forces; and in its comprehension of the latter the communist world was well ahead of the West, using Western errors and the hang-over of imperial ways to devastating effect. Nor can the West opt out of its involvement in the Arab world for, with oil consumption increasing at the rate of twelve per cent annually, it is the only area with reserves capable of meeting the massive defence and industrial needs of Western Europe. Alternative sources of power cannot alter the situation in the foreseeable future. For the West working relations with the Middle East have become a matter of survival.

In Europe the 'war of ideas' is an unfashionable concept. Many believe the Cold War disappeared with Khrushchev. The Russian presence in the Middle East is seen in primarily military terms. Yet democratic contempt for the word 'ideology', together with an unfortunate propensity to foresee the methods of a future war in terms of the last, may be exposing the West to great danger. The Russians have not given up for a moment their marxist ideology and their world purpose; and to hope that they have reverted to some sort of nineteenth-century political imperialism is wishful thinking. The Americans are no clearer about all this than the Europeans. A recent issue of Moscow's *International Affairs* notes with satisfaction that Henry Kissinger, Nixon's adviser, in his book *American Foreign Policy*, 'presents ideology as a sort of "infantile disorder" which ends with maturity'.

The underlying lesson has not been drawn from the events of the 1950's when Dulles and Eden, bent on containing Russia, launched the Baghdad Pact which was to have been an extension eastwards of the defensive system provided in Europe by NATO. From the start the Pact drew Arab opposition for it was seen as a re-appearance of the Western presence, a far grimmer reality to the long-occupied Arabs than any future threat from Russia. When in 1956 Eden sought to dislodge Nasser by promoting an Israeli attack on Egypt as a cover for embarking with France upon the ill-fated 'Suez' intervention, the Arabs' worst fears materialised. Earlier the same year anti-Baghdad Pact pressure in Jordan forced the resignation of Glubb.[1] Two years later, the pro-Western monarchy in Baghdad itself was overthrown by Kassem.

The Baghdad Pact was an anti-communist device. Nasser opposed it. So Washington and London concluded Nasser was pro-communist, a misapprehension which supporters of Israel have often been happy to sustain. In fact Nasser's hostility to the Baghdad Pact was nothing to do with his attitude to communism, but sprang from the antipathy he and the growing middle class leadership of the Arab world felt towards pacts and bases with their 'strings' and veiled control over the junior partners' governments.

Failure to differentiate between Arab nationalism and communism has long been the cause of misunderstanding and miscalculation, and the fact that the Communist Party is recognised in no Arab country still comes as a surprise to many in the West. Of course, Russian military instructors and economic experts are numerous in Egypt, but Egyptians will challenge the critical Westerner to name any instance when aid was not first sought from the West —and refused. Israel, anxious to hold on to the backing of

5

America, stresses the danger of a 'red' Middle East. But it is probable that there are as many committed communists inside Israel as there are in all the Arab countries put together; and certainly it cannot be doubted that Russian military aid to Egypt is the result not of Arab partiality for the doctrines of Marx, but of Arab fear of Israel's military might.

These are considerations that need to be weighed by anyone concerned to understand Arab Socialism, the political ideology of more than half of the fourteen independent Arab States.[2]

Perhaps the essential starting point for the Westerner intent on understanding other parts of the world, is the abandoning of the assumption that Western ways are necessarily for universal application, irrespective of differing cultural backgrounds. The Arabs, although they are marching towards their goals helped by Western progress and research, are also seriously hampered, they feel, by a long legacy of misunderstandings and disservices at the hands of Western politicians and their armies and administrators.

As Sir John Glubb has pointed out in his series of books on the Arab era, there has been an abysmal ignorance of Arab history even amongst educated people in the West. School children learn about the Greek and Roman empires, but then follows the void known as the 'Dark Ages'. For the West, it was dark; but for the Arabs this was their golden age, when they dominated the 'developed' world of that time.

Centuries later, with the opening of the Suez Canal a little over a hundred years ago, Western interest began to turn seriously to the Middle East and Britain established a form of protectorate over Egypt which had long been a dependency of the Ottoman empire. Parliament buildings were built and the forms of two-party government set up, but always the British High Commissioner ruled from off-stage; and at moments of crisis for British interests, as when Sir Lee Stack was murdered in 1924 and eighteen years later when Rommel was advancing in the Western Desert, the British representative, Lord Allenby in the first instance, Sir Miles Lampson in the second, was quick to by-pass parliamentary process, and with a show of force, bring King Fuad and his successor King Farouk speedily to heel.

The latter episode when, in April 1942, armoured cars lined up before the royal palace in Cairo to reinforce the British ambassador's demands proved to be a turning point in Egyptian history. For on that day of humiliation was born the Free Officers movement which produced Nasser.

When the Second World War was over and as hundreds of thousands of war-weary Allied troops were queuing up to get home from the Middle East and to shake off the sand of the desert, the British government served notice on Washington that Britain could no longer be looked to for the containing of Russian pressure in that area. As a result the embryo C.I.A. hurriedly began recruiting Arabists.

Predictably, and before long, the Americans became interested in the underground Free Officers, and in particular in a major who had distinguished himself in the Palestine war of 1948, Gamal Abdel Nasser. This man seemed to Washington, at that time, to be a leader who could become strong enough in the Arab world to make peace with Israel. This would heal this open wound which kept alive the bitter Arab resentment at the betrayal of the Palestinians —a grievance which Russia was already beginning to use effectively against the West.

In July 1952, following a breakdown of law and order in Cairo, the corrupted and irresponsible King Farouk, who symbolised foreign influence over Egypt, was deposed in a bloodless and completely successful coup. Two years later the figurehead of this revolution, General Naguib, gave way to its actual leader, Nasser, who became president.

The officers who carried through the 1952 revolution were passionate nationalists. For the most part they were not politically or ideologically minded. Most were men of religious conviction. As has often since been the pattern in Asia and elsewhere in Africa, the army provided a means for a new middle class leadership to emerge in a society where hitherto a land-owning oligarchy of ruling families had dominated affairs.

The Revolutionary Council was at first disposed to pack off King Farouk and his entourage and then hand back government to the politicians. But it became swiftly plain that the power of the landowners, who had always blocked reforming legislation under the old régime, would prevent any real change if the army withdrew. So while some of the promising younger officers went off to study for degrees in technical subjects, the group around Nasser set themselves to the tasks of government, to the building of national morale and to the carrying out of some cautious social reforms.

The only major reform, however, which was achieved before the interruption of the Suez war of 1956 was the first land re-distribution. This followed a decree limiting land ownership to two hundred *feddans* (acres), with an additional one hundred if the owner had two or more children. It was a significant step. For the striking feature of Egypt's agriculture, its basic industry, had always been the glaring inequality of the system of land ownership.

Ever since the days of Mohamed Ali and the subsequent khedives who ruled Egypt under the Ottoman empire, the greatest part of the agricultural area of the country was owned by the ruling dynasty and by a small minority of pashas, often of Turkish or Albanian origin. As late as 1950, the statistics show that, whereas only one in ten of the population owned any land at all, some ninety great landowners had estates each worth more than two million pounds.

This minority class who owned such a considerable proportion of the country's resources naturally enjoyed a monopoly of political power; it had succeeded in keeping agriculture free from taxation of any sort and had successfully blocked every attempt to limit ownership or to control rents.

With this background it is not surprising that the revolution soon began to move in the direction of social reform, and that the elimination of feudalism was the first objective. In any case, the exiling of the King immediately confronted the new government with the task of disposing of the extensive royal estates which he left behind.

Given the conditions in Egypt at the time, the emergence from the Nasser revolution of some form of socialistic régime was a foregone conclusion and the pragmatic socialism which began to emerge was a natural development of the passionate nationalism of the revolution whose architects were determined to give self respect and dignity to the masses of their countrymen and to rescue them from their conditions of squalid poverty, ill health and hopelessness.[3]

In this task they enlisted some outstanding civilians. El Ruwad (The Pioneers) was a society which had been formed in the 'thirties by a group of university professors and professional men with the aim of developing the social conscience of the intelligentsia, and particularly of the younger generation in Egypt. They organised clubs and settlements in the slum districts of Cairo and Alexandria. They were a remarkable and disinterested body of people, and no less than nine of their members served as government ministers in the years immediately after the Revolution. Dr Abdo Sallam, until recently Minister of Health of Egypt, was one of the early members of El Ruwad.

For Nasser political factors overshadowed social factors during the 'fifties; but his book *The Philosophy of the Revolution* makes it clear that from the start he was deeply aware of social issues. It was not, however, until the publication of the 1961 labour laws that the theoretical aims and content of his Arab Socialism began to be clarified and expressed as government policy.

The National Charter of the following year, a new and abridged translation of which is published in this book, carried the process further.

During the Second World War, Allied troops in their thousands swarmed through Cairo. Almost all were completely oblivious of the hostility their presence provoked among the Egyptian military and the nationalists. Few knew that some of the nationalist leaders were prepared, at that time, to go along with the German National Socialists if it would hasten the end of decades of British occupation. Other Egyptians, on the other hand, looked to Moscow as the key to the future. Still others, however, dreamed of achieving a distinctively Arab form of socialist society incorporating the principles of Islam.

The men who take up the story now were among the latter. Both Abdel Moghny Said and Samir Ahmed in their different fields have worked to help that dream become reality. What they write throws light on the authentic Arab Socialism which has emerged from the Egyptian revolution and which has been adapted and adopted in much of the Arab world.

Little has previously been written in English about Arab Socialism and even less by Arabs who have themselves taken part in its development.

* * *

In September 1970, Gamal Abdel Nasser died and was succeeded as president of Egypt by his comrade-in-arms Anwar Sadat.

Just eight months after this, in May 1971, just before William Rogers, U.S. Secretary of State, visited Cairo to discuss possibilities of settlement of the Arab-Israeli conflict, a major shake-up of government ministers took place. The Vice-President, Aly Sabry and six ministers including Sharawy Gomaa, the Minister of the Interior, and General Fawzy, the War Minister, were dismissed by Sadat.

This action forestalled a probable coup against Sadat by an element amongst the leadership which, whatever its motives, was certainly not known for its concern for the more humanitarian aspects of Egypt's social revolution nor for its strength of Islamic conviction such as had characterised Nasser and many of his closest colleagues.

Even before the dismissal of Sabry and his set, President Sadat had spoken of the need 'to codify the revolution' and he had called for work on a 'permanent constitution' to define 'everything in our life and to clarify the landmarks, structure, guarantees and boundaries of our future society'.

Then, after the sweeping ministerial changes, the National Assembly set up a committee of fifty to redraft the constitution and ruled that its work must be completed by the national day, 23 July, only two months later—a proviso suggesting that new principles were not being sought but rather a new enthusiasm to make the existing system work effectively.

Although Sadat seems less preoccupied than was Nasser with Egypt's political role in the Arab world as a whole, he clearly shares his predecessor's determination to develop a distinctively Arab form of socialist society within Egypt. And he made it clear to the National Assembly that, despite his dismissal of Sabry and other prominent figures in the Arab Socialist Union, he had no intention of abolishing Egypt's single political party. Instead it would be 'reformed', and a committee of a hundred was set up to carry through this task. From the composition of this committee it is clear that, once again, 'reform' was to be a matter more of changing emphasis rather than of altering the broad principles.

At the same time as all this, Hussein Shafei, one of Nasser's closest friends and one of the original Free Officers who carried out the 1952 revolution, was appointed sole Vice-President.

Before the end of May, President Podgorny hurried to Cairo to make sure the Soviet investment in Egypt was not going to be jeopardised by all these changes, but the fifteen years' treaty of friendship that resulted did not, in fact, alter in any material way the relationship that had previously existed between Egypt and the Soviets.

Arab Socialism remains, as before, a self-conscious pragmatic, ideological phenomenon jealous of the integrity of its origins in Arab nationalism and in Islam.

This book is not an apologia for Arab Socialism. Rather have its authors set out to present facts that may not generally be known. Their aim is to contribute to better understanding between peoples. It is the story of a struggle against formidable odds; of a continuing struggle; and of a struggle which, if it can be won without forfeiting the goodwill of the West, may greatly contribute to world stability.

W. L. M. CONNER

Chelsea, S.W.3.

NOTES AND REFERENCES

[1] Lieut.-General Sir John Glubb ('Glubb Pasha') who commanded the Arab Legion in Jordan from 1938-56.

[2] Egypt, Iraq, Libya, Sudan, Syria, Algeria, Yemen (Sana) and Yemen (Aden) have socialist governments. Saudi Arabia, Kuwait, Jordan and Morocco have traditional monarchy-type governments; as have Bahrein and the other seven Gulf States which are soon to become independent. Only Lebanon and Tunisia have systems somewhat resembling Western type parliamentary democracy.

[3] Under the régime of King Farouk the infant mortality rate was almost 1 in 3. By 1969 it had been reduced to 1 in 10.

Part One

ARAB SOCIALISM : ITS THEORY AND PRACTICE

I

The Earlier Socialists

At first sight the idea of socialism seems simple and has
many attractions. People imagine a socialist state and envisage the fulfilment of all their hopes of justice, security
and lasting peace. A closer look, however, reveals various
schools of socialist thought and different approaches to its
application. For many are the roads which lead towards
the socialist ideal.

During the second half of the nineteenth century there
were many different voices to be heard including those of
the co-operative socialists, anarchists, Marxists, social demo-
crats and Fabians. Then there were the socialist experiments
after the First World War, the most notable being the
Soviet experiment of October 1917.

Today there is in the contemporary world a variety of
marxist socialist experiments, most of them named after
the countries in which they are being worked out. These
are referred to, at least in socialist circles, as 'The Soviet
Socialist Experiment', 'The Chinese Socialist Experiment'
or 'The Yugoslav Socialist Experiment'. It is not acceptable
to speak, for example, of 'Soviet Socialism'.

When it comes to Arab socialism, the case is different.
This is because the Arab socialist experiment has not declared marxism as its basis. It may learn from the marxist
scientific method, as it is hoped it may increasingly from
Western socialist thinking and experience, but its foundations have been firmly laid in the Islamic cultural heritage.

17

It was after the First World War and the rise of the Soviet Union as the first socialist country that socialist ideas began to take hold in parts of the Arab world. Progressive writers began to propound the principles of socialism, and socialist or communist parties, either open or underground, began to appear in the Arab countries and notably in Egypt and Lebanon.

The Egyptian Socialist Party was established in 1921 by a small group of socialist intellectuals. Unfortunately their action was premature. Circumstances and conditions were unfavourable, as they had neglected to elaborate a solid ideological basis which fitted local conditions and needs, and a socialist trend of thought in the country had not been created.

Hosni El Orabi, son of a cotton exporter, who had inherited a fortune from his father, financed the new party, and it soon succeeded in establishing strong links with the trade union movement for whose backing it hoped, along with that of the working class as a whole. The party succeeded in gaining the nominal support of twenty-two out of the thirty trade unions existing at that time, and with their help and patronage the first Egyptian Federation of Workers was established in 1921, with a total membership of about forty thousand. However, the intellectual and administrative foundations were inadequate and the party disintegrated in less than four years.

Historians have found difficulty in getting reliable information about this party. No documents are available, and Hosni El Orabi died before writing his memoirs. Nevertheless the following facts emerge from his private talks with the author and others during his lifetime.

The Egyptian Socialist Party, having affiliated itself to the Third International in Moscow, found itself bound by conditions existing in Egypt at that time. For instance, the certain of its resolutions which were not applicable to decision to adopt as the name of the party 'The Egyptian Communist Party' merely for reasons of solidarity and without considering the implications was a serious error. Almost all the intellectual members resigned from the party leaving El Orabi alone with the rank and file worker members and an international organiser, one Rosental, a rich Jew who was later found to be more concerned for the interests of Zionism than for those of international communism. So it was that the workers became identified with the Egyptian Communist Party and the Egyptian Federation of Workers came to be regarded between the wars as being pro-communist.

Another error concerned the general strike which was to be launched in 1923 all over the world following a resolution adopted by the Third International. The Egyptian Communist Party was in no position to launch such a strike at that time, having to compete for the support of public opinion with the national liberation movement which was absorbing all thoughts and efforts. In addition the Egyptian Federation of Workers was still in its infancy and, having no reserve funds, could not run the risk of starting a general strike which might continue for several days. Another factor which made the general strike undesirable was that after the declaration of national independence and the issuing of the 1923 Constitution, general elections brought into power, for the first time in Egyptian history, a popular democratic cabinet headed by Saad Zaghloul, the great national leader of that time. This popular government was faced with hostility and intrigue both from King Fuad and the British High Commissioner.

In view of all this, Hosni El Orabi was given liberty by Moscow to stop the strike should he think it advisable in the event of an appeal to do so from Zaghloul's popular government. The general strike took place, and the expected appeal was immediately made. All the strikers responded to the appeal and returned to work, with the exception of some of the Alexandria workers who were persuaded to stay on strike by Rosental, the international organiser. The Wafdist Government had to use force in getting the Alexandria strikers out of three factories which they had occupied, but the evacuation took place without casualties. Leaders of the strike, as well as leaders of the party, were arrested and put on trial. The party was not dissolved and the restrictive measures taken by the Zaghloul government were relatively mild. As for the Federation of Workers, no action was taken against it, but the Wafdist Party thought it wise to take it under its own patronage.

Reconsidering its relation also with the Egyptian trade union movement in the light of these events, the Wafdist Party decided to appoint a political figure, Abdel Rahman Fahmy, as president of the Federation of Workers. He was chosen because of his previous experience with the trade unions as the organiser of the Wafdist 'underground' in Cairo during the immediate post-war period.

This first Wafdist government, however, was soon overthrown, following the assassination of Sir Lee Stack, the British Inspector-General of the Egyptian armed forces, in November 1924. The government which followed, led by Ziwar Pasha, was a mere tool in the hands of the King and the British. It dissolved the Communist Party and put a complete ban on all communist propaganda, agitation or organisation. El Orabi was sentenced to five years in prison, while Rosental found himself ousted from the communist underground and denounced by the Third International.

When El Orabi came out of gaol he began to publish a weekly magazine *Ruh Al Asr* (*Voice of the Era*) but it was banned after about six months, and throughout the 'thirties socialist activity was almost at a standstill. However, the appearance of *Al Tatawor* (*Evolution*) as a monthly paper in January 1940 gave notice that Egyptian socialists were beginning once again to re-organise themselves. Several communist and socialist underground organisations were formed, the most important of which were 'Hadito' (Arabic initials for 'The Democratic Movement for National Liberation'), and 'Dar Al Abhath' ('The League of Scientific Studies'). These underground organisations were weak both ideologically and in their militancy. They limited their activities to study circles and indoor debates, and had no direct contact with the working masses. Absorbed in intellectual argument and scattered in rival organisations, they became pre-occupied by their own conflicts. Some of them also came under the Zionist influence of Jewish intellectuals who were in some cases very rich, and whose motives were undoubtedly suspect. Their influence appeared in the anti-patriotic and anti-religious tendencies which dominated the thinking of some of the cells. Similar trends were to be found in some of the communist circles in other Arab countries during the 'forties and 'fifties. During and after the Second World War, communists in Syria, Iraq and Lebanon propagated the idea of co-operating with Jewish workers and farmers in Palestine against the British Mandate—a naïve idea in view of the Zionist auspices under which these Jews had immigrated into Palestine.

Tendencies such as these had made the communists most unpopular and considerably slowed the spread of socialism, bringing it into conflict with the new current of Arab nationalism which was beginning to flood over the Arab world as the Second World War came to an end. The establishment of the Arab League in 1945 was one indication of the growing strength of this movement. Political parties proclaiming Arab unity began now to appear in many of the Arab countries and some of these parties were also socialist. It was at this time that the term 'Arab Socialism' was used for the first time to describe a political philosophy as distinct from marxism as it was from other forms of socialism.

More than once this development was to lead to clashes in different parts of the Arab world between communists and nationalists as, for example, under Abdel-Karim Kassem's régime in Iraq; and again, following the union between Egypt and Syria in 1958, when the Syrian Communist Party was declared illegal and its leader, Khalid Bagdash, had to flee from Syria seeking political asylum in Bulgaria.

For tactical reasons, differences were at times dropped in the interests of a joint struggle against a common enemy, but the underlying conflict remained.

The godless and materialistic aspects of communism make it particularly unacceptable as a belief in the Arab world where there is still a profound respect for moral values and where the dramatic decline in faith that both the Communist and Western blocs have undergone in the last decades has not been experienced to anything like the same extent. Unconvinced by communism no less than by the 'affluent society', some of the most thoughtful and responsible leaders in the Arab lands are seeking how their distinctive Arab socialism can make a fuller and more positive contribution to the moral re-armament of international affairs.

2

Origins and Principles of
Arab Socialism

The conflict between the cause of Arab unity and international marxism naturally affected the development of
the Arab socalist movement, and brought to the fore the
whole question of what Arab Socialism really stood for.
Questions were raised in socialist and political circles far
beyond the Middle East. What exactly was Arab Socialism? When was the term first used? Where lay its roots
and origins? Was it an Arab version of Nazism? Was it
an Arab adaptation of marxism? Or was it, in fact, a
largely original movement with its own ideology, of which
the terms of reference lay in an Arab and Islamic cultural
heritage far older than Western socialism?

During the 'fifties, Western political commentators tried
to establish a relationship between Arab Socialism and
Hitler's National Socialism. The surge of national feeling
that accompanied the last years of the independence
struggle, together with the passionate call for Arab unity
doubtless had something to do with this. In addition, some
of the German technicians who came to Egypt at this time
had Nazi backgrounds; but the ceaseless propaganda directed against Nasser, Arab nationalism and Arab Socialism
in the world's press by those who sympathised with Israel,
was undoubtedly a major reason for the success at this time
of the pro-Nazi misconception.

The concept of Arab Socialism actually existed for many centuries before modern Arab nationalism came upon the scene. Its roots were planted long before Marx. They lie deep in the soil of Islam and in the cultural heritage of the Arabs.

All the great monotheistic religions were cradled in these Eastern Mediterranean lands which have always been the home of the Arab people. The impulse towards social emancipation is found in all these religions, but it is perhaps most developed in the precepts of Islam. The Quran makes it clear that, as well as setting up moral standards as a basis of decent behaviour and better human relations, religion must bring help to the poor and improve the living standards of the masses. In previous revelations the social message was simple: 'Do not exploit; be charitable; practise unselfishness.' In Islam, for the first time, an economic theory of equal opportunities and fair distribution was outlined.

Without becoming too theological, it is possible to explore the social and economic implications of Islam and to identify some of the Islamic principles which have influenced contemporary Arab socialist thought.

In the first place, Islam teaches that God is concerned not only with moral and ethical reform, but also with social emancipation and economic conditions. Thus God-fearing man is inevitably involved in the moral aspect of the 'class struggle', in so far as the exploited masses are on one side and the over-rich, the tyrants and the arrogant are on the other. Thus the Quran outlines a 'scientific' theory of socialism.[1]

The Quran provides a basis for a moral interpretation of history; an interpretation which is deeper and broader than that of Karl Marx because it covers both the moral and material aspects, while that of Marx concentrates entirely on the material aspect being greatly influenced by the materialistic evolutionary philosophies of his time. Religion is not the opium of the people. The great religions aimed at a classless society, where equality, justice and prosperity would prevail. In their principles and particularly in Islam, which Marx completely ignored, we can trace much that pointed towards socialism.

In his book *Islam in Modern History*[2] Wilfred C. Smith writes 'The Islamic enterprise has been the most serious and sustained endeavour ever put forward to implement justice among men; and until the rise of marxism was also the largest and most ambitious. Yet it differs from marxism in that for Islam every mundane event has two references; is seen in two contexts. Every move that a man makes has an eternal as well as a temporal relevance. While marxism is entirely materialistic, Islam's material outlook is based on moral standards and values, in the light of which all historical events must be judged.'

According to the general economic and social principles given in the Quran, there should be a reasonable minimum standard of living for each individual, as well as a maximum level of affluence, and in between these two limits every individual is free to gain according to his ability.

The minimum margin should be such as to provide decency and adequacy. It should be based on recognition of a common right to enjoy natural resources and to have access to the benefits of scientific and technical progress. Such a minimum living standard should increase in proportion to increases in the productive capacity of society as a whole. It must also be increased so as to meet new needs arising from technical progress. The aim of sufficiency or adequacy for everyone is affirmed in the Quran in simple words but carrying the strongest meaning: 'God gives sufficient to the man who serves him.'[3] The requirement to remedy material inequality and level out extremes of wealth and poverty is underlined throughout the Quran, and themes such as the following often occur:

When you give, give from the best of what you have.

God favours a full life for everyone.

Never forget that everyone has an equal right to a share of life's gifts.

Above the minimum living standard, acceptable in relation to that of society as a whole, individuals are allowed to better their lot according to their ability. The more they work and produce, the more they will have. Economic grades are permitted, but they must be related to merit so that they do not develop into parasitic social classes. 'And for all there will be ranks derived from what they do.'[4] Such economic grades are necessary for the functioning of human society, and they provide much needed cadres of authority and responsibility. They are the natural outcome of man's varying abilities. All this is developed in the Quran.

In Islam, work is an honour, a right and a sacred duty. Every citizen shall work according to his ability and do his utmost not only in his own interest but also in that of the community as a whole.

Everyone shall be paid in proportion to his work, and no man should be allowed to live on the yield of private property without himself doing any work. 'No laden one shall bear another's load. And man should only have that for which he makes effort.'[5]

In a modern society, which functions on principles of division of labour and specialisation and with a high degree of interdependence, grades of income and responsibility are clearly necessary, but those in higher grades should have to pass tests of competency, and the taking of personal advantage from high position and the wronging of those in lower positions should be checked. 'God it is who has placed you as viceroys of the earth, and has exalted some of you in rank above others, that He may test you through the responsibility which He has given you.'[6] Here it is implied that unjust rulers are not to be tried only by God in the hereafter, but are also subject to trial in the life of the world through juridical safeguards and democratic supervision.

A maximum level of income is advocated by Islam in order to protect society. Such a maximum must obviously be relative and has to be flexible. Islam, however, has laid down the principles to be taken into consideration in fixing such a maximum in accordance with prevailing conditions.

One such principle is that wealth should not be allowed to accumulate in the hands of the privileged few to the extent that they could exploit and dominate. 'That it become not a commodity confined to a limited circle of wealth.'[7]

Such accumulation would lead to luxury, easy living and waste, and bring degeneration and decline.

Hoarding is denounced as harmful to the community, because it keeps money from fruitful circulation. It is as harmful as allowing irrigation water into one's land, and preventing it from going to the lands of others. 'They who hoard up gold and silver and spend them not in the way of God, unto them give tidings of a painful doom.'[8]

Indeed, in many revelations of the Quaran, Muslims are commanded to spend because spending is in the interest of the community. All wealth belongs to God, the creator of all things. Man is but a trustee. 'Believe in God and His messenger, and spend of that whereof He has made you trustees; and those of you who believe and are liberal will be richly rewarded.'[9]

Man shall spend not only in the time of prosperity, but also in the time of adversity and depression. Spending in the time of depression, including public expenditure and the expansion of public works, is recommended as a means of hastening the return of prosperity. He who spends altruistically is promised benefit from his spending. 'And whatever good thing you spend, it will be repaid to you in full, and you will not be treated unfairly.'[10] And again: 'Those who spend their wealth in God's way are like a grain which grows seven ears, in every ear a hundred grains.'[11]

The fixing of a maximum level of income is seen as a means of re-distributing the national income. It takes from those who have more in order to give to those who have less. Direct and progressive taxation, together with free public services, are but a modern application of this principle, which is confirmed by the saying of Mohammed: 'God taxes the rich among Muslims to provide sufficiently for the poor. The poor would not suffer starvation were it not for the misdeeds of the rich.'

Islam calls not only for redistribution of wealth, but also for a more equitable allocation of leisure. Leisure nowadays is considered a human need as well as an economic commodity sustaining growing recreational and touristic industries and services. Islam has long insisted that it should be equitably shared.

Individual property and private enterprise are permitted in Islam, but such permission is subject to self-imposed limitations intended to prevent exploitation and protect the interests of the community as a whole. If such limitations fail to materialise then intervention on behalf of the public can become necessary. Here lies the basically different approach of Arab Socialism to nationalisation from that of marxism. For Arab Socialism, nationalisation is a means, not an end. Private ownership from the Islamic point of view is not an absolute and sacred right, it is a social function. It should not be separated from work, which is an honourable duty as well as a moral obligation. If private ownership evades its social function and develops

28

into a tool of man's exploitation of man, it should be controlled in the name of God, who is viewed as the absolute owner of everything, because the creator of all things. 'To Him belongs everything in heaven and on earth.'[12]

The next chapter gives a short survey of the progress Arab Socialism has made in Egypt.

NOTES AND REFERENCES

[1] This question is dealt with in greater detail in *Islam—a Progressive Faith for a Dynamic World* by Abdel Moghny Said (Al Karnak, Cairo).

[2] Wilfred C. Smith: *Islam in Modern History* (Princeton, U.S.A. 1957).

[3] Quran 39:36

[4] Quran 46:19

[5] Quran 53:38-41

[6] Quran 9:34

[7] Quran 59:7

[8] Quran 18:7

[9] Quran 57:7

[10] Quran 2:272

[11] Quran 2:261

[12] Quran 55:2

AUTHOR'S NOTE: The difficulty, acknowledged by Western Arabic scholars, of arriving at an adequate translation of the original Quranic Arabic must be appreciated.

To the Christian, God's revelation was centred in the *person* of Jesus. His actual words were part only of the divine message. To the muslim, God revealed himself in the Word. Mohammed was 'His Messenger' only. Thus the words of God, transmitted in Arabic to Mohammed, and preserved in the original, have a unique significance for the muslim.

3

Arab Socialism in Practice

The Egyptian revolution, which resulted from the bloodless coup of 23 July 1952 when members of the Free Officers movement deposed King Farouk and opened the way for Nasser to become president, was the most momentous political event in the history of modern Egypt. It was also, however, a social and economic turning point of the first importance since, in abolishing the monarchy and the feudal landowner, it opened the way for socialism. From the beginning, the leaders of the revolution had emphasised the social consequences of national liberation and had stressed that the struggle of the Egyptian people was to be directed not only against colonialism, but also against the feudal nature of their own society and the abuses of capitalism. The objectives of the revolution always included the establishing of political democracy and social justice. The building up of a strong national army was also seen as essential in order to protect the newly-gained independence and the benefits that would follow it.

Towards these ends certain measures of social significance were immediately taken. These were the reform of land tenure, the abolition of the civil titles of 'bey' and 'pasha', symbols of a class hierarchy, the removal of the monarchy as an institution and, later, the bringing in of the new constitution of 16 January 1956.

The 1956 Constitution formalised the socialist nature of the state. It took into account for the first time in Egypt the social and economic rights of the citizen in addition to his civil rights and personal freedom. The part of social and economic planning was also emphasised in the constitution, as a means of directing economic activity towards the general interest of the people. In February 1960, the banks and insurance companies were nationalised, a step which was found essential in order to control savings and investment, and to enable full comprehensive planning to be effective.

Previous nationalisation laws had, of course, been issued, such as the nationalisation of the Suez Canal in July 1956, and the nationalisation of British and French concerns immediately after the tripartite attack of November 1956, but the motive at this time was more nationalist than socialist. It was not until July 1961 that nationalisation was extended on a large scale as part of a programme of socialist transformation.

In 1961 eighty important industrial and commercial companies were nationalised. Later the same year a further eighty companies, mainly in the agricultural services sector, were half-nationalised, the government appropriating fifty per cent of their capital. A third law followed forbidding the owning of shares of total value over 10,000 Egyptian pounds by one person in any of a group of a hundred and forty-five named companies. Shares in excess of this were taken over by the State who compensated the owners in debentures guaranteed by the Treasury. The maximum legal limit of private land ownership was also lowered the same year from two hundred to one hundred feddans per family.

The nationalisation laws mentioned above were accompanied by the introduction of a system of profit sharing and participation in management. It became law that twenty-five per cent of the total annual profits must be allocated to workers and employees and distributed in the following manner: ten per cent payable in cash, five per cent allocated to social services, particularly workers' housing, as agreed upon by management and the trade unions; ten per cent allocated to central social services.

Workers' cash shares in profits began for the first time to be distributed in 1962 and in the early months of 1963. The average annual cash payment accruing to an ordinary worker was about fifty Egyptian pounds. The distribution of workers' cash shares in profits has been continued in the years following and was not interrupted by the war of June 1967.

Participation in management had first been introduced two years earlier in the form of joint committees on the staff level and joint councils on the 'shop floor' level. A further and more effective step was taken in this field on the occasion of the ninth anniversary of the 23 July Revolution, when the composition of boards of directors in companies and concerns was reorganised. It was laid down that members of these boards should not exceed seven in number and one of these had to be elected by the staff and another by the workers.

Immediately after the announcement of this law, President Nasser emphasised its importance as a significant step in Arab Socialism stating that 'Ours is a humanitarian socialism which believes in the individual and his role in life. We cannot look at the worker in the way we look at a machine. We should enable him to participate in management.'

During the next two years the success of workers' participation in management was evaluated. In practice, weaknesses were found which hampered the effectiveness of the new system. Board meetings were held in many cases at too long intervals. Top management was in some cases reluctant to co-operate with the elected members on the board. President Nasser, who was keen on the success of this new experiment in management, took a lead in exposing such negative attitudes and in recommending action for their remedy.

In an address to the workers of the Nasr Motor Company during his visit to the plant in Helwan in July 1962 he said, 'We have introduced workers' participation in management. We are going to increase the percentage of elected members representing the workers on the board of directors. We expect such boards to acknowledge the full rights of labour representatives to express freely their opinions. If they venture to intimidate or dismiss any of the worker-members on the boards, this will be considered as sabotage of the social structure we are in process of building.'

Several laws and presidential decrees were issued in October 1963 with a view to consolidating workers' participation in management, this being seen as a step towards the eventual development of worker-management as the ultimate objective. The general outcome of these laws and decrees may be summarised as follows:

(a) Membership of the management boards was enlarged to nine members, four of whom were to be elected by the personnel of the concern.

(b) The board of directors was compelled to meet at least once every month.

(c) A sub-committee of the board was set up in each company consisting of three members, one of them at least to be appointed from among the elected members on the board. This sub-committee was to deal with workers' personal and welfare problems.

(d) Elected members on the boards, as well as other workers on boards of various trade union organisations were protected against dismissal or suspension from work. Their dismissal or suspension from work became a matter for the judicial authorities.

In spite of such legislation, there are naturally still many difficulties and anomalies, and probably the bureaucratic mentality is the greatest of these. Bureaucracy is the common disease of all socialist experiments, and the Arab experiment is no exception. Serious action will have to be taken to reduce it to a minimum. If it is left to develop, it could create a new class of 'feudal bureaucrats'. In spite of political orientation and management training courses, the harnessing of the bureaucratic tendency remains a major problem.

Labour legislation before the 23rd July revolution was of a very limited sort and did little for the real protection and welfare of the worker. Owing to the political domination of the great land-owners of the pasha class, agricultural workers were excluded from the scope of most labour laws. As was to be expected, this discrimination against the agricultural workers was ended by the fall of the feudal régime.

The Land Reform law of September 1952 was a landmark in Egypt's history for it extended the right to organise to agricultural workers for the first time. It fixed their daily working hours and set up committees to fix minimum wages. Also, the registration of trade unions, which had given government power to recognise or not to recognise a union, was abolished. For the first time in Egypt the right to freedom of association and the right of labour to organise for the purpose of collective bargaining were recognised.

In 1956, a committee was set up to revise and regroup all existing labour laws in a new labour code which would conform with the general principles of the constitution. After the union between Egypt and Syria in 1958 another joint committee representing the two regions was set up for the same purpose. Certain improvements in working conditions, annual paid holidays, sick leave and maternity benefits were among the results which they achieved.

In July 1961, a presidential decree was issued reducing working hours to forty-two per week. A statutory minimum wage of twenty-five piasters (pence) a day was fixed, doubling the minimum wage of 1950. In November 1962, a ministerial order was issued for the formation of 'joint committees on dismissals'. These were formed in concerns employing fifty or more workers, to review all dismissal orders made by management. Any dismissal order was henceforth considered null and void unless it had been referred to the committee for perusal. The committee, composed of three members representing the local labour office, management and the local trade union, was empowered to refer to relevant documents and to hear appeals from any or all parties concerned.

The first social insurance system called the Insurance and Provident Funds Plan was introduced in 1955. Two separate funds were established, one for insurance and the other for savings. The insurance was limited to compensation in event of total disability or death. The savings scheme was designed to provide for a pension or gratuity payable to the worker at the termination of his period of service. In 1959, a new law was issued extending insurance to workers in industry and commerce against partial disability, industrial accidents and occupational diseases. A further improvement took place in 1961 when both insurance and saving schemes were amalgamated into one which was called 'Old Age, Disability and Dependants Insurance'. At a later stage, a more comprehensive health insurance was introduced, providing for medical care, including surgical operations, hospitalisation, and supply of medicines. In October 1965 came the introduction of unemployment insurance.

The nationalisation laws and the pushing forward of labour and social legislation again raised questions in Egypt as well as in international circles as to what was the theoretical basis of the Egyptian socialist experiment. On what ideological foundations were the Egyptians building their new socialist system? Were they following the socialism of Marx?

To mark the first decade of the revolution, President Nasser presented, in 1962, before a congress of peoples' representatives, a National Charter which set out in ten chapters an answer to these questions.

The Charter defined the new Egypt's objectives and the methods by which they were to be achieved, and it embodied much of Nasser's own political philosophy. It was proclaimed and adopted as a theoretical basis and an ideological guide for the Egyptian socialist experiment.

The Charter makes it clear that 'valid solutions to the problems of one people cannot necessarily be found by importing the experiences of another'. It also affirms that 'socialist action can no longer be expected to follow literally laws formulated in the nineteenth century', a statement that is unquestionably an indirect reference to marxism. The Charter, on the other hand, later emphasises that previous socialist theories must not be rejected categorically through prejudice.

The five 'proclamations' of aim outlined in the Charter underline the basic principles of the 1952 revolution and provide basic guidelines for its continuation, and in so doing they clarify a great deal.

The first two are concerned with the sustaining of the 'will to revolution' and with the 'revolutionary vanguard' whose function is to give effect to the national purpose and ensure that the nation's leadership is directed towards its fulfilment.

The third 'proclamation' emphasizes 'the ability of contemporary man to influence history'. The fourth provides for the right of criticism and states that the Egyptian revolution should keep 'a mind open to all human experiences for from these it can benefit and to them it can contribute as it avoids rigidity of attitude.' By open-mindedness, which is the condition of new discovery, the Egyptian socialist experiment is in a position both to receive and to contribute.

In the fifth and last 'proclamation' the Charter affirms the Egyptian revolution's 'unshakeable faith in God, his prophets and his sacred messages which he passed to man as a guide to justice and righteousness'. This firm statement of faith is an open rejection of the materialistic aspect of marxism.

The Charter goes on to affirm the importance of moral and religious values in modern progressive societies and states that these values are 'capable of guiding man, of lighting the candle of faith in his life and of bestowing on him unlimited capacities for serving truth, goodness and love'.

If it were not for this great difference between the approach of Arab Socialism and that of marxism to religion and spiritual values, the gap between these two ideologies would look somewhat narrower. The Charter welcomes the concept of 'scientific socialism', seeing it as 'the best means of finding the right way to progress', and again as 'the only way to economic and social progress'. The people's control over the tools of production is strongly stressed, but such control can be achieved by planning, and 'it does not necessitate the nationalisation of all means of production or the abolition of all private ownership'.

As regards the major framework of the country's economic life, the Charter stipulates that railways, roads, ports, airports, dams, major sea, land and air transport undertakings, and public utilities generally should be owned by the state.

In general, heavy industries and mining should also

come under public ownership, though here, in certain cases, controlled private ownership may be allowed. In the field of light industry private ownership is appropriate so long as monopoly control does not arise, and here competition with the public sector has a role in stabilising prices.

Foreign trade falls largely under state control. All import trade must be carried on within the framework of the public sector, but private capital is encouraged to take part in export trade. Where possible, and in order to preclude fraudulent practices, the public sector must handle three-quarters of the export market but the private sector is to be encouraged to shoulder responsibility for the remaining quarter.

As regards internal trade, the public sector should take over at least a quarter of this.

Banking, also, must be a public service and capital, being a national asset, must not be left in the hands of private speculation. In addition, insurance companies were taken over by the state in order to give the maximum protection to this major element of national savings.

In the matter of land ownership there was to be a clear distinction between two kinds of private ownership; that which encourages profiteering and is opposed to the spirit of the revolution, and that non-exploiting ownership which plays its part in the service of national prosperity while providing reasonable profits for the owners themselves. The agrarian reform laws of 1961 limited individual ownership to one hundred *feddans* (acres). The spirit of the law was that this limitation should apply to a whole family, and not to the individuals within it, so that the creation of large family blocs could be prevented. The Charter called for this spirit to be implemented within the coming eight years, and urged that families who were evading the law should sell the land in excess of the legal limits in cash to the agricultural co-operative societies or to others.

As regards ownership of property, the taxation of buildings and the laws limiting rents have placed it beyond the reach of profiteers. The increase in publicly-owned housing built by co-operatives will tend also to militate against profiteering in this field.

Such was the scope extended to public ownership in the Charter of 1962. In the following years further nationalisation took place, affecting flour and rice mills, large bakeries, river transport and shipping. Since then, the public sector has increased as new factories have been set up. In 1970, wholesale businesses were nationalised, and the percentage of the economy, if agriculture be excluded, which is now state-owned is approximately eighty per cent of the whole. It is the biggest percentage achieved by any of the Arab socialist countries, and, in this respect, comparable with certain socialist régimes which have pursued the marxist course.

In 1969, maximum individual land ownership was decreased to fifty feddans, while that of the family remained at one hundred feddans as previously decided by the Charter. Still, however, private ownership prevails in agriculture. As it states in the Charter, 'the Arab application of socialism in the domain of agriculture does not call for nationalisation. It believes in individual ownership of agricultural land, within limits that would not allow for the return of the large landowner class'. This realistic attitude came out of the lessons and experience of some of the socialist countries, where public and collective farms have not shown encouraging results.

Retail trade is left in private hands. Craftsmen and those working on their own in small industries and services form together a group which is called 'Non-profiteering national capitalism'. This group is not only allowed to co-exist with the public sector, but it is entitled to join the socialist Alliance of the Working Peoples which consists of farmers, workers, soldiers and intellectuals.

In fact, a small private sector is allowed to exist and function as a competitive stimulant to the public sector. This is clearly emphasised in the Charter which states that 'the maintenance of the role of the private sector alongside that of the public sector renders control over public ownership more effective. By encouraging competition within the framework of general planning, the private sector constitutes an invigorating element in the economy'.

Some Arab marxists have expressed reservations about this formula, but their objections seem to be dogmatic and theoretical and little related to the realities of practical experience.

Any survey of Arab socialism would be incomplete were it not to recognise the special role played by Gamal Abdel Nasser. For Nasser's leadership not only made possible the Arab socialist experiment in Egypt, but his personal contribution both to its theory and to its practical expression was pre-eminent.

He did much to ensure the integrity of the experiment by laying its foundations upon the principles to be found in Islam. At the same time, he was concerned to keep developments in the Arab world in touch with modern socialist thought elsewhere. To a degree he respected marxism as the inspiration of much that was of social worth in today's world, but he had profound doubts about its materialistic basis. The term 'scientific socialism', which he used in the National Charter, was open to misunderstanding and the Arab marxists took it to refer to marxism. When Nasser was asked what, in fact, he meant by 'scientific socialism' he replied: 'I mean scientific socialism —but not materialistic socialism.'

Gamal Abdel Nasser was a man of simple origins, son

of a post-office clerk from Beni Mur, a village in Upper Egypt. Born in Alexandria in January 1918, he had a restless and hard childhood. His mother died when he was eight years old.

He had an early experience of violence when, in his teens, he was slightly wounded during the suppression of student demonstrations. Later he took part in the political activities of the Wafd Party and of Ahmed Hussein's Socialist Party and at this time came to realise the need for a more effective approach to the task of changing the situation in the country. He became convinced that demonstrations and slogans would not bring independence.

He decided to join the Military Academy specifically to prepare himself for a positive part in the freeing of his nation from a medieval-type monarchy largely under foreign control. He was commissioned in 1938 and from this time on the revolutionary underground in the armed forces began, later to develop into the Free Officers movement.

In the Palestinian war of 1948, Nasser, by then a major, distinguished himself in the successful counter-attack at Falluga. After the war the military underground grew in strength. The appalling corruption and inefficiency in high places brought to light by the war spurred the recruiting of new members and the prospect of a revolution spear-headed by the army began to take shape. On the 23 July, 1952 the revolution came. King Farouk was deposed and the monarchy was abolished.

Nasser was a man of deep human feeling as well as a man of vision and action. His *Philosophy of the Revolution*, which was published after the revolution, in 1954, reveals this; and this explains in part why it was that the revolution was carried through almost without bloodshed. During the phase of drastic changes which followed, no serious internal conflicts took place in spite of differences

41

among the leadership. At various times certain of the original members of the revolutionary council withdrew, some to reappear again later on the front line, but purges were avoided. From the outset it was a popular revolution and for this reason was not typical of military coups d'état. The intention to de-militarise the government of the new order was declared and carried out by Nasser himself and down to the present time the army has continued to keep out of politics. The resilience and stability of the régime undoubtedly owe much to this fact.

It is true that there were occasions when Nasser took harsh measures against individuals and groups, but this he felt bound to do for the protection of the new order. He was often caricatured in the world's press as a ruthless dictator but those who knew him personally, both his fellow countrymen and foreigners, were invariably impressed by his integrity, humanity and by his dedication to the regeneration of his people.

Nasser gave the Arabs back their self-respect and, after centuries, their independent nationhood. His other outstanding achievement, perhaps the more remarkable in a man of military background, was his work on a formula for a constitution, adaptable to the Egyption situation, which would allow, and indeed promote, a progressive advance towards a fully democratic society.

He believed that socialism could only work if it were implemented by a people imbued with a truly socially-developed outlook; and of this outlook there was in Egypt at the time of the revolution an acute, if understandable, shortage. It was no easy task that he and his colleagues faced in laying the basis for a socialist state at home, compatible with the ideals of Islam and of democratic freedom —involved as they also were in a state of war with Israel and, at one point, with France and Britain also.

The European-type political parties and parliamentary

system had been completely discredited under the old régime, so a start was made by establishing a popular mass organisation, the National Union. This body, set up in 1957, provided the first real bridge between the people and the government. Basically it was a chain of elected committees formed throughout the country and ranging from the twenty-five governorates at the top down to village level. Two members of each committee were elected to represent it on the committee on the next higher level. These committees were to supplement, cross-check and criticise the work of the appropriate governmental executives on each level. It was the beginning of a process of decentralisation and laid the framework for a popular 'pyramid' base to the central government.

In 1962, Nasser's National Charter set up the Arab Socialist Union to replace the National Union and develop its role. Now, alongside the elected village and town committees, there were to be A.S.U. committees representing the urban population in the factories, businesses, civil service departments and elsewhere. On each committee now, on every level, half the seats were to be allocated to farmers so that the major element in the nation's population would be assured of representation.

Nasser, and others such as Hussein Shafei of the original revolutionary council upon whom the president leant heavily, had no wish to create a single party in the sense that the Communist Party existed, as a closed élite, in communist countries. Membership of the Arab Socialist Union was open to any citizen over eighteen years of age who had not been specifically debarred on account of offences against the state.

This nation-wide political structure was designed to inspire civic consciousness and to promote responsible participation by the people in the government of their country. In order to achieve its aims it needed to be supported by a vast programme of educational and ideological training, and the Workers Educational Organisation was founded in 1961 to launch such an undertaking. Its task was to raise the cultural and intellectual level of the people, to train leadership in the field of organised labour, to promote political understanding and initiative and to relate socialism to the Islamic heritage.

The organisation runs more than fifty centres throughout Egypt for basic courses and adult education and operates six institutes for more specialised courses. The youth organisation of the Arab Socialist Union has also its institutes and seminar centres.

Finally, the National Assembly—re-named by President Sadat in May 1971 the 'People's Assembly'—was inaugurated in 1964. Each of 175 constituencies in the country was to elect two members and one of these two was required to be a worker or peasant farmer.

Such, in outline, was the path taken by Nasser in his quest for a means to develop a form of 'direct' democracy whereby the people's voice could be heard and whereby an ever-growing number of citizens could participate in shaping their nation's affairs.

4

Democratic Influence of Islamic Concepts

The early appeal of socialism in Europe undoubtedly owed much to the failure of the traditional political systems to provide economic freedom for the mass of the workers. The proposition that true political democracy could only be built upon foundations of economic equity was a strong one. Unfortunately, what was promising in theory has not borne fruit in practice. Some socialist experiments have found it necessary to impose restrictions upon civil rights and the basic freedoms of the individual under pretext of protecting the socialist revolution against its enemies. Such restrictions, in theory applicable only to counter-revolutionary elements, have often been extended in practice to affect the lives of the ordinary people, and even, on occasion, those of sincere socialist leaders.

Transitional periods have tended to become prolonged as progressive leaders acquired a vested interest in maintaining emergency restrictions, making use of them to suppress criticism. Such dictatorial tendencies, masquerading behind the seemingly innocent slogan of 'the dictatorship of the proletariat', are wholly unacceptable but it is not an easy phase beyond which to advance. In our own time movements to 'democratise' socialism have frequently been crushed by force, sometimes even by invasion across national frontiers.

What is the approach of Arab socialism to this delicate problem of extending the frontiers of individual liberty in society? Can Arab socialists find in the application of their own Islamic principles a satisfactory solution?

Democracy is not a matter of casting a vote in a periodical election. The ballot box must be undergirded by a democratic attitude to life permeating everyday affairs and affecting human relationships and attitudes.

In addition to a form of parliamentary system, there need to be other democratic institutions. Organisations through which the people can participate in the running of their own affairs, such as village and town councils, joint councils and committees of industry, parent councils for schools and people's committees in local government. In the Arab socialist experiment, the aim is that the citizen shall be enabled, as far as possible, to exercise his democratic rights directly and with the minimum intervention by the professional politician. It is a concept of democracy deeply rooted in Islamic principles and much dependent upon the spirit of community and brotherhood inherent in Islam. Indeed those who believe in Islam and are genuinely attempting to live the quality of life for which it stands should, in fact, have an approach to life and to their fellow citizens which is truly democratic in spirit.

The ideal Islamic society would consist of citizens who, having chosen their faith, have become liberated from every allegiance other than that which they have undertaken towards God. A society which truly lived and applied Islam could not but be free and democratic. Its citizens would be, as Mohammed put it, 'as equal as the teeth of a comb'.[1] No discrimination whatsoever is envisaged in this classless society. When Muslims practise their communal prayer, they pray in equal rows and in complete harmony. There are no reserved places for those in higher positions. Governors, leaders or men of authority should

46

not be cheered. 'Mosques are only for God, so bow down to no one along with God.'[2]

Mosques are usually called by muslims 'God's homes'. They are not regarded merely as places of worship. They can be used equally for appropriate communal purposes, such as teaching, lecturing and arbitration. They may also function as local forums where questions of general interest may be discussed, not only after the *Gomaa* or communal prayer, but whenever necessary. The weekly public speech, which is given before the Friday prayer, usually deals with the topics of the week and it may develop into a limited debate or a popular discussion after the prayer. The Khalif, the elected Islamic leader, might himself give the speech in the mosque where he prayed and participate in debate on equal terms. The great Khalif, Omar Ibn El Kattab, is on record as having accepted gracefully contradiction from an unknown woman in one such public discussion. The Khalif, which simply means 'the successor', although exercising the authority of a governor, was expected to live as a simple man without privileges, following the example set by Mohammed, the first ruler of the Islamic state. His simple humility was widely acknowledged and held in high esteem by many Western writers. Sir William Muir in his book *The Life of Mohammed*[3] writes 'a practical simplicity prevailed over his life. His habit was to do everything for himself. He helped in the household duties, mended his clothes, tied up the goats, and even cobbled his sandals. He was to all comers easy of access, yet he maintained the bearing and dignity of real power'. Thomas Carlyle writes of him : 'No emperor with his tiara was obeyed as this man in a cloak of his own making.' Abu Bakr, Mohammed's successor, said in his first speech after his nomination and election, 'I have been appointed to lead you; it is an appointment which does not mean that

I am the best of you. Help me if I do well. Check me if I do wrong.'

Those who are interested in Islamic democracy in practice, may study in more detail the experience of the early muslims under the rule of Mohammed and his two successors Abu Bakr and Omar Ibn El Khattab. During this period the political implications of the Islamic faith were worked out and a democratic experiment unique in history resulted . The Khalif was elected by means of a plebiscite in which both men and women had the right to participate. Citizens of the Islamic state had the right to elect their rulers and there was provision of checks should they deviate from Islam or act wrongly. Neither Mohammed nor his Rashid successors were ever accused of acting harshly or rigidly. They were true to the Divine command to Mohammed, 'You are not to act like a warder over the people'.[4] They maintained a basis of consultation with their people, in line with various Quranic injunctions, such as 'consult with the people upon the conduct of affairs'.[5] It was accepted that those who had authority were under an obligation not to abuse it. The principle of what is morally right was taken as the basis of policy, and the social conscience implicit in Islam found expression in the relations of the government with the citizen as well as in relations between the citizens themselves.

According to Islam, muslims have the right to check their rulers if they act unjustly, and to replace them if they persist in persecution or flagrant injustice. To accept tyranny is as much a crime as to tyranise and, a true muslim must fight tyranny wherever it exists. 'Sanction is given to those who fight if, in fact, they have been wronged; and God is indeed able to give them victory'.[6] If a citizen fails in the attempt to resist tyranny and to protect his freedom where he lives, he is instructed to seek refuge elsewhere. To humiliate oneself by accepting tyranny is a punishable offence: 'The angels shall say to those who put themselves in a subject position, when they die: "In what were you engaged?" They will reply: "We were oppressed in the land." The angels will then say: "Was not God's earth spacious enough for you to have emigrated? For such as you, your habitation will be hell, and it is an evil resort.'[7] In no other faith is freedom valued so highly.

The islamic democratic ideal, in the early period, was simple and direct. It was made possible by a common faith which was lived by the people in their everyday life. This prevailed over their human activities and relationships. It affected relations between the governor and the governed, the master and the servant, parents and sons. The government apparatus was simple and very limited as compared with that of modern times. There were nothing like political parties at the time of the early muslims, but provision was always made for 'the other point of view' to be heard. People were free to express their opinions and, however they might differ, everyone was expected to respect the opinion of others. Different schools of thought existed and enjoyed complete freedom. There was none of the suspicion that goes with spying. 'You believers, shun suspicion. Suspicion is a crime. And do not spy or criticise behind one another's back.'[8]

The suspicion of a police state has a deadening effect. This fact, which many nations have learned from bitter experience under dictatorships and totalitarian régimes, was clearly recognised by Mohammed: 'If the prince makes use of spying in ruling people, he will soon corrupt them.'

The term 'direct democracy', which is often used to describe Islamic democracy, has been recently used in some socialist countries, notably by the Yugoslav socialist leader Kardel. By 'direct democracy' is meant a system under which the citizen exercises his democratic rights in a direct way, neither under the political tutelage of one party, such as in the Soviet one-party system, nor through the intermediary of either a governing or an opposition party, as in the case of the multi-party parliamentary systems.

This recent concept of 'direct democracy' is not original. It was to be found in early Islamic democracy.

In Egypt, the Charter of 1962 followed these Islamic lines. 'We must always bear in mind that, for the individual, freedom is the foremost condition to be achieved. Slaves can carry loads of stone, but only free men can soar high among the stars. Freedom of belief is the only firm basis for faith. Without freedom, faith turns into fanaticism which is a barrier shutting out new thought. In freedom alone is man inspired to move forward and to catch up with those who are ahead of him. Freedom of speech is the first condition of democracy. The sovereignty of law is its final guarantee.'

The Charter asserts that 'political democracy could not be separated from social democracy. No citizen could be regarded as free unless he was free from economic exploitation, with equal opportunity to have a fair share of the national resources, and his mind free from anxiety and insecurity.

The Charter rejects the idea of dictatorship of the proletariat, stating that 'political democracy could not exist under the domination of any one class. Democracy meant the sovereignty of the entire people. The inevitable and natural class struggles could not be ignored or denied, but their resolution could be arrived at peacefully and with the aim of creating national and class unity'.

In seeking to avoid the dangers of a one-party system, the Egyptian socialist experiment has evolved a mass political organisation, linked to elected councils and to the workers' organisations such as the trade unions and the co-operatives. This is the Arab Socialist Union. Membership is open to every citizen over eighteen years of age who has not been deprived of his political rights for offences against the state or offences involving dishonour. There are two classes of membership: 'working members'. who must be literate, and who are eligible for office within the union, and 'external members' who have only voting rights. Within the first year after its foundation in 1962 the Arab Socialist Union's membership exceeded six million members, or one-fifth of the country's total population. The Socialist Alliance of the Working Peoples in Yugoslavia may be considered the nearest to the Arab Socialist Union among political organs in other contemporary socialist countries.

The general principles which the Charter emphasised as the basis of the Arab Socialist Union may be summarised as follows:

1. Adequate representation of those elements forming the majority of the population to be ensured. Farmers and workers to get at least half of the seats on committees and representation bodies at all levels, and also in the House of Representatives itself.

2. The elected popular councils to be in a position to exercise supervision and control over their corresponding executive departments in government, making it possible for the will of the people to affect national action. In local government also there should be a gradual but sustained transfer of authority from the state to the people, who are often in a better position to assess their problems and vote for the right solutions.

3. The popular organisations, especially co-operatives and trade unions, to play an effective and influential role in promoting democratic procedures. They can act as a vanguard force in the various fields of national activity. Their relation to the Arab Socialist Union is a relation of associa-

tion and not of integration, and this independence enables them to look after the interests of those they represent the more effectively.

4. Collective leadership, the supremacy of the law, and provision for criticism to be maintained as the most effective safeguards against the concentration of power in the hands of ambitious power-seekers.

The Charter recommended the creation of a new advisory body within the general framework of the Arab Socialist Union, which would be composed of men of background and qualifications who could help ensure that government policy met the needs of the masses, and continued to strengthen the ideas and aims for which the revolution stood.

The nature and purpose of this 'advisory committee' have been much discussed. Does it have independent authority? Is it a secret or an open organisation? What is its present membership? President Nasser dealt with such questions on various occasions, making it clear that 'the advisory committee' is not a secret organ, nor a dominant force within the Arab Socialist Union. It is rather the Union's vanguard for ideological thought and guidance. It is in no sense a political party.

Some of the Egyptian marxists expressed the view that the absence of a strong party was the main cause of defeat in 1967. They started a campaign calling for the immediate formation of 'The Party'. The Party would solve all our problems!

The present author was one of the socialist writers who stood firmly against this. There was no valid reason for blaming the Arab Socialist Union. The June War took place in Sinai, a desert area without villages and towns, If the hostilities had been extended to village and town in the Nile Valley, it would perhaps have been possible then to evaluate the role of the Arab Socialist Union in organising and leading popular resistance against the enemy.

These particular marxists were apparently trying to take advantage of the desperate situation after the military defeat. Their campaign, however, was doomed to failure. The Egyptian people would not accept under any circumstances the idea of having a one-party system under the faded slogan of 'dictatorship of the proletariat'. This slogan has little appeal, in an era grown hostile to the idea of dictatorship, after the bitter experience of the many countries which suffered under the rule of Fascism. Almost all countries which took the course of socialism after the Second World War called themselves 'People's democratic republics' as an expression of their adherence to democratic ideas and of their antipathy to the concept of dictatorship.

The Soviet Union itself, incidentally, has put aside the words 'dictatorship of the proletariat' and has adopted the more acceptable slogan of 'sovereignty of the working class', a step which was deemed necessary during the period of reaction against Stalinism.

REFERENCES

[1] Quran—13
[2] Quran—72,—18
[3] Sir William Muir: *The Life of Mohammed* (4 vols. 1858-61, Smith and Elder).
[4] Quran 88: 22
[5] Quran 3: 159
[6] Quran 22: 39
[7] Quran 4: 97
[8] Quran 45: 12

Part Two

ARAB SOCIALISM: ITS PLACE IN WORLD IDEOLOGIES

M. SAMIR AHMED

This section is an abridgement of a longer work entitled 'Nasser's Arab Socialism; its place in world ideologies' written by Samir Ahmed in 1966 under the auspices of the Centre for International Affairs at Harvard University.

5

Roads to Socialism

Socialism may be described as an institutional pattern in which control of production is vested in a central 'popular' authority and in which the economic affairs of society belong to, and are decided by the state rather than by private individuals.

Many socialists, however, believe that socialism is more than an economic system whereby inequalities are banished by eliminating the distinction between the 'haves' and the 'have-nots'.

The manner in which this is done, they consider, is of primary importance if essential human values are to be preserved and not destroyed in the process of achieving the economic ends.

On one side, of course, there are the marxists who contend that socialism can only be built through 'class conflict'. They see in every country unpatriotic feudal and semi-feudal forces representing the bourgeoisie and often linked with foreign interests remote from the general good of the people. Such people are prepared to co-operate with the 'imperialists' and thus are, in communist eyes, the natural and irreconcilable enemies of true socialism.

Democratic socialists believe, on the other hand, that communist methods on occasion distort agreed socialist ideals to the extent even of negating some of the principles which Marx himself preached. 'Equality' can open the way for a rigid economic and political hierarchy ruling in the name of the dictatorship of the proletariat. The principle of humanity can be regarded as expendable in the interests of some future millennium. The scientific, objective approach to economics and politics can bend before the demands of dogma and short-term expediency.

In her penetrating study of African socialism Margaret Roberts does not deny the profound debt democratic socialists owe to Marx's ideals and to his analysis of capitalism. But she does not accept that his prescriptions are universally applicable. She believes the fundamental quarrel is with the marxist concept of the perfectibility of the classless society and the withering of the state. This she describes as a 'fanatical illusion that has justified communist cynicism and intolerance and the sacrifice of its humanity'.[1]

Her outlook, to some degree, reflects that of many leaders of the emerging states who today regard themselves as socialists but not marxists.

Orthodox communists, of course, maintain their objection to democratic socialism. Referring to Western socialists, the Soviet ideologist, Professor I. Potekhin, wrote in 1963:

'They speak in favour of socialism, but interpret it in such a way that socialist ideas become a veiled apology for the capitalists' way of development. Propagation of false socialist theories, like the "democratic" socialism of the British Labour Party, has created much confusion about true socialism.'

But whatever the communist conception of true socialism may be, it has become increasingly clear that, as the split between Russia and China has grown and particularly since the death of Stalin, there has been a growing acceptance of the fact that there are many roads to socialism, and among these roads, Arab Socialism is one which, if little known and publicised, is nevertheless advancing year by year upon carefully laid foundations.

During the first years after the 1952 revolution, President Nasser was largely pre-occupied with foreign affairs and with the practical realities of running a country from which the existing feudal leadership had suddenly disappeared. In spite of this, however, he published his short but illuminating statement of political faith, *The Philosophy of the Revolution*, in 1954.

But it was not until seven years later that a comprehensive statement was made on the thinking which lay behind the social and economic legislation of the new régime.

Nasser's theory of socialism was set forth in the address and statements he made to the Preparatory Committee convened in November 1961 to lay the groundwork for a National Congress of Popular Forces. The congress was held in May, June and July 1962 for the purpose of considering the draft of the president's 'socialist manifesto': The Charter of National Action.

The National Charter lays down a detailed programme of action for the decade to follow, a period envisaged as one of transition towards the establishment of socialism in Egypt. At the same time it provides a comprehensive and authoritative basis for the study of Nasser's theory of socialism.

REFERENCES

[1] M. Roberts in A *Socialist Looks at African Socialism* (Stanford University Press, USA).

9

The Human Factor

In the Charter and throughout the other writings on Arab
Socialism, there recurs an underlying attempt to balance
material and economic with humanitarian factors and to
take into consideration the situation of the individual
citizen. For example, the reduction of the scope of private
enterprise is seen not as a doctrinaire matter of principle
directed against private ownership as something in itself
bad, but as a necessary means of curbing the self-interested
and haphazard behaviour of private owners upon whose
voluntary public spiritedness reliance could not be placed.

Nasser never saw the nationalisation of some of the
means of production as incompatible with ownership of
private property and reasonable rights of inheritance. In
the case of agricultural land, he was definite that the particular circumstances, ability and history of the Egyptian
fellah or farmer made nationalisation of the land a highly
injudicious proposition.

On the question of the 'class struggle', Nasser did not
see this as an inevitable element in the development of a
socialist society, nor did he believe in the dictatorship of
the proletariat or of any other class. Indeed the idea of
dictatorship of any sort, as a means of controlling the
social order, was wholly unacceptable to him.

Rather than see a trend towards any one class becoming
all-powerful to the exclusion of other sections of the population such as the intelligentsia or private business, Nasser

aimed to encourage an alliance between all the different 'forces' or elements in the community. The Charter describes it as a 'democratic interaction between the dynamic forces of the population, which are the peasants, the workers, the armed forces, the intelligentsia and private business'.

Nasser was not pre-occupied with society as an abstract concept but as the mass of individual human beings living on the soil of their homeland. He saw man as the end and object of social action; and the aim of socialism to be the well-being of the citizen. The establishment of socialism, he saw as a means and not an end in itself.

In his own mind Nasser seems to have regarded as the most important accomplishment of the revolution, the restoration of a sense of self-respect and of moral and physical dignity to his countrymen. This explains his refusal to concentrate on building heavy industries to the exclusion of consumer-goods industries. He would not sacrifice the well-being of the present generation for the hypothetical happiness of future generations. He felt deeply the privation the masses had suffered over centuries and was not ready to allow mobilisation for industry to delay the meeting of the people's consumer needs.

Just as the welfare of the citizen and the health of society are interrelated, so too he saw the social and political revolutions within the nation to be mutually complementary. And it was the social revolution, made possible by the initial political revolution with its somewhat limited objectives, which, in turn, opened the way for a second and more long-term phase of political development.

Socialism and democracy Nasser saw to be complementary. Without socialism he believed that democracy provided a cover for economic dictatorship; but without democracy, socialism stood to lose its two most important characteristics, namely equality and humanity. Underlying his whole approach to planning and development there was always an emphasis upon the rights and welfare of the individual citizen.

7

The Pragmatic Socialism of Nasser

Nasser was completely frank about the fact that, when the *coup d'etat* against the notorious régime of King Farouk succeeded in July 1952, he found himself with a successful revolution on his hands but with no doctrine, no specific programme, and with no political organisation upon which to rely.

In saying this, however, it must not be forgotten that there were in Nasser's mind at this time two important concepts. The first was the necessity of 'two revolutions'— the political and the social; and the second was a statement of objectives which had circulated among the Free Officers before the revolution and were known as 'the six principles'.

Nasser often enlarged on the theme of the two revolutions that Egypt had to go through. In *The Philosophy of the Revolution* he wrote: 'Every nation on earth goes through two revolutions. One is political, in which it recovers its right of self-government from an imposed despot or an aggressive army occupying its territory without its consent. The second revolution is social in which the classes of society struggle against each other until justice for all citizens has been gained and conditions stabilised.

'Other nations have preceded us along the path of human progress and passed through the two revolutions, but not simultaneously. Hundreds of years separated the one from

63

the other. In the case of our nation, it is going through the two revolutions together.'

The 'six principles' of the 1952 revolution also expressed the need for both a political and a social revolution. Later on, these principles were incorporated in the 1956 Constitution and appeared again in the Charter of National Action of 1961.

They can be summarised as follows:

The eradication of foreign control, direct or indirect, over any part of the country's life; the abolition of the feudal system of land tenure, of commercial monopolies and of control by private financial power in government; the establishment of equality for all before the law; the building of a strong national army; and, finally, the inculcation of sound democratic principles throughout society.

However, these six objectives, in Nasser's words, were no more than 'landmarks along a difficult road', or 'banners under which the revolutionary throngs marched'. They represented neither a code of revolutionary action nor a programme of radical change.

In the absence of a clear-cut programme, Nasser had to resort to improvisation at the outset. 'We had the courage, at the beginning of the revolution, to declare that we had no theory, though we did have clearly-defined principles', he said later. 'We declared that we would proceed, by trial and error, to construct a theory. We proceeded thus for ten years.... We would study in the meantime; we would diligently try to learn.... But we would also act. We continued to say that we would make mistakes; and we continued to admit that we had no theory. But despite everything, we were able to take action and to achieve something, to get things done ... and, as a result, we are now heirs to an experiment and to the practical results of some eleven years. This has furnished us with a basis for theory.'[1]

It would not be wholly correct to conclude that, in the absence of a theory or a programme of action, Nasser's progress towards socialism was haphazard. For the six principles were a guiding light. Every act was measured in advance against the yardstick of these guide lines, and action was taken only if it would bring nearer the goals towards which they were directed.

Nasser's first act of nationalisation came in 1956. Faced with the sudden withdrawal by the United States and British governments of their offer to help finance the building of the Aswan High Dam project, Nasser moved immediately to 'Egyptianise' the Suez Canal in order to use the canal revenue as an alternative source of finance for the Dam.

With Egypt's population increasing at a rate of 2.5 per cent per year, the Dam had become a matter of survival for millions; for besides its hydro-electrical potential, its stored waters were to make possible an increase of 30 per cent in the cropable area of the country. So the revenue from the canal was seen as a way to make the continuation of the Dam possible. The act of nationalisation was done as a specific answer to a human need.

Nasser tended to scorn abstract speculation and theory. To him, theories were of value only when they were rooted in experience. When constructed in the abstract, in advance of experience, he regarded theory as worthless, even harmful.

The Syrian Baathist party has probably the oldest coherent body of socialist theory in the contemporary Arab world. It dates back to 1946 and its aim is a just and equitable society in which extremes of wealth and poverty do not exist. The Baath Constitution calls for the redistribution of land holdings among the citizens on a just

65

basis, for the nationalisation of utilities and large industries, for sweeping improvement of wages and working
conditions and the provision of old age insurances, free
medical care and free compulsory education through the
secondary level. Gamal Abdel Nasser's 'Arab Socialism',
while not a direct outgrowth of Baathist ideology, is very
similar in its economic and social theories. But where
Nasser has succeeded in applying socialism, including the
achievement of all the targets listed under the Baath Constitution, the Baath has expounded the theory of socialism
only and put it into practice only hesitantly.

Although there are similarities between some of the ideals
and aims of the Baathists of Syria and Iraq and Nasser's
Arab Socialism, there is no evidence that Nasser received
from Baathism any guidance as to the practical implemen-
tation of his aims. The contrary would probably be nearer
the truth, and it was undoubtedly Egypt which defined
and first carried through the process of socialist transformation which set an example for all other Arab socialists
to follow.

An interview of President Nasser by the Egyptian newspaper, *Al-Ahram*, in February 1960, provides insight into
his thinking about Egypt's development at this time.

'I have heard,' he said, 'of those who consider our
socialist régime a compromise; who believe that since we
have adopted a political stand mid-way between East and
West, our social system must therefore be a compromise
between communism and capitalism. Then again, I have
heard of those who claim that because we have developed
our own social system, we have come to believe in it,
merely because it is not an imitation of anyone else's.

'I see nothing farther from the truth than these sugges-
tions. Firstly, because the political neutralism we uphold
is not a mid-way stand between East and West, but rather
one of non-involvement in the Cold War between two

camps, with the definite desire to keep our opinion on international matters impartial and independent so that we can lend it to the side of justice wherever we find it. Secondly, even if it were possible in the Cold War and in international affairs, to take an intermediary or middle-of-the-road stand, it would be impossible to take such a stand in the realm of social beliefs. The Cold War is a struggle between two camps; we should strive to keep away from its currents until we make our decision. But social beliefs are a more subtle matter. They are a matter of the heart, the mind, and the soul. Social beliefs do not grow roots and develop on their own. They grow roots when they are genuinely close to men's hearts, minds and souls. A nation's heart may be said to be its hopes for the future; its mind, its present; its soul, its past. You cannot take a midway stand between your heart, mind and soul.

'The interaction of a nation's heart, mind and soul, in a sense, yields its social ethos. It is the authentic expression of the particular circumstances in which a nation finds itself.'

This statement well illustrates the pragmatic approach out of which Arab Socialism has grown and continues to grow. It may be that if Arab Socialism has so far produced but few theoreticians it is because it has come about more through the practical necessity of the hour than by pursuit of an academic principle.

REFERENCE

[1] Proceedings of the unity talks between Egypt, Syria and Iraq (Cairo: Al-Ahram Press, 1963).

8

Rifaat and Distinctive Features of Arab Socialism

A recurrent theme, not only of Nasser but of many Egyptian commentators, was that Arab Socialism does not limit itself to the social and economic aspects of life. Kamal Rifaat,[1] a close associate of the late president and one of the original Free Officers who had planned and eventually carried out the 1952 revolution, has commented on the distinctive features, as he sees them, of Arab Socialism.

Socialism, he believes, is more than an economic system; it is also an attitude of mind embracing all the activities of the community. Socialism to him is a path which has a beginning but no end, because it marches with the times, changing with the times, evolving with their evolution and varying with actual conditions and circumstances.

National feeling he places foremost among the distinctive features of Arab Socialism. For the latter was born and grew up in the first half of the twentieth century—a period of growing reaction to colonialism and to those leaders within the colonised countries who were the agents of the foreigner.

Rifaat also stresses that Arab Socialism derives a special character from the area's 'moral and spiritual traditions, national history and early civilisation and from the temperament of the Arab people.' He points also to the stress laid upon human and individual needs and underlines the emphasis upon the community with all its different constituent elements which militates against theoretical principles which might operate for the benefit of any one element or for that of the impersonal state itself.[2]

While recognising the impact of material and economic factors on the historical development of communities, Arab Socialism believes in the influence of the moral and spiritual factor as well. Thus socialism and religion are held to be perfectly compatible. In point of fact Nasser often said that the religion of Islam was the first to enjoin socialism.

Arab Socialism also rejects the deterministic interpretation of history. It holds that the individual plays an important role in shaping history, not that history shapes the individual.

Arab socialism does not automatically follow any world 'bloc' or tendency. It believes non-alignment can issue in positive policy. It is concerned more with national than international and 'universalist' political doctrines.

As for the role of the state, its status is held to be that of the community's servant, entrusted with protecting it and ministering to all its classes rather than that of 'apex of the socialist community'. It is a state representing the whole people and not any one class. Gradually, the state will change the social order so as to impart greater freedom, dignity and self-respect to the people as a whole.

More recently Arab Socialism has been evolving a policy of 'centralisation of planning and decentralisation of execution' in order to encourage healthy competition and personal initiative.

Perhaps the most remarkable feature of Arab Socialism is the way it is working out an alternative to the one-party system which characterises the political life of the Communist bloc.

According to Kamal Rifaat, Arab Socialism has little

faith in either the one-party or the multi-party systems. 'On the one hand,' he writes, 'we find that from the multi-party system arises the division of the community into various classes, each of which tends to constitute a political party to defend its own interests regardless of the wider interests of the community.... As regards the one-party system, this party tends to become part of the mechanism of the state, and the mass of the people becomes subjected to the command of this exclusive party within which authority is often concentrated in the hands of a small group. This conflicts with our concept of socialism as based on the theory that the mass of the people, and not the party, should exercise a leadership role.'[3]

The Arab Socialist Union, a political organisation but not a party, is an attempt to establish a means through which the leadership of the state can have a popular base, and by means of which a two-way process of communication between leaders and led can be conducted. It was established in 1961 as the 'highest political authority' in the country and in this capacity it was to determine the permanent constitution of the country. Its founding statute defines the Union as the 'formation embracing and representing all the popular forces—farmers, workers, soldiers, intellectuals and private holders of national capital'. It is the supreme instrument of Egypt's socialist democracy.

Nasser took pains to explain that the Arab Socialist Union was not a political party. During the period of 'socialist conversion', originally seen as lasting for a decade from 1962, no political parties were to be countenanced. If they emerge afterwards, they will have to arise within the framework of the Union and not outside it. The banning of political parties during the conversion period was seen as necessary to protect the early stages of the revolution.

The Arab Socialist Union, meanwhile, was to be the

means through which the popular view as to the method and pace of socialisation could be gauged.

REFERENCES

[1] At present (1971) U.A.R. Ambassador to the Court of St James.
[2] Kamal Rifaat, *Arab Socialism* (S.O.P. Press, Cairo, 1962).
[3] Kamal Rifaat, *op. cit.*, pp. 16-17.

9

Socialism in the Developing Countries

Today, when the advance of technology is beginning to affect large areas of Asia, Africa, the Middle East and Latin America, the leaders of the nations variously described as 'new', 'uncommitted', 'emerging' or 'developing', hold in common many ideas about the type of society they want to build. For example, when it comes to the drive towards economic and industrial development they are, for the most part, reluctant to follow the model of the United States, the European nations or even of Japan, each of which achieved their industrial revolution under the auspices of private enterprise.

The nationalist leaders of emerging states, with the exception of some of those in Latin America, are united in rejecting the capitalist method of development as slow, unsuited to their conditions, and above all discredited by past association with imperialism. In this, it must be admitted, Lenin's theory of imperialism has been remarkably successful in colouring the emerging people's outlook towards Western capitalism. It has been truly said that the 'albatross of history' hangs around the neck of the West as it bids for the ideological understanding of the developing world. So, in the view of the new nations, rapid economic growth can only be attained by 'socialist' methods, although the meaning of this, in practice, is rarely defined in detail, nor agreed upon among its advocates.

For the majority of these new states, during the period

of economic take-off, when the conditions for self-sustained growth were either non-existent or just beginning, private investment more often than not was unable or unwilling to shoulder the responsibility of economic construction, even if it had been politically feasible. This was exactly the situation in Egypt when Nasser took over. A divergence between the requirements of public interest, on the one hand, and individual and minority interests on the other, predictably arose, and this made inevitable a 'command economy' based on planning by a central authority.

Reluctantly it has to be acknowledged that if underdeveloped countries are to grow rapidly economically, they may have to accept, certainly at first, some limitation of democratic participation in political affairs.

Among those who advocate socialism, capitalism is rejected for moral as well as economic reasons. The socialism of the developing nations is seen to be aiming at the establishment of a society based on justice rather than profit, on planning rather than the blind operation of market forces, and on industrialisation as opposed to the acceptance of an economy geared to the production of raw materials for foreign manufacture. This is how socialism is regarded by nearly all the leaders of Asia, Africa, Latin America and the Middle East.

Marxism, in one form or another, has had a tremendous impact on the thinking of Afro-Asian leaders. There is, however, little acceptance of the principle of class war. Socialism of a non-doctrinaire sort, idealistically implying state action for the general welfare of all, has remained a simple ideology easily understood by the masses, while undiluted communism appears to have gained comparatively few committed adherents in this area of the world.

To equate the nascent socialism of developing countries with the communist bloc, therefore, is to ignore a fundamental and recurring factor in the thinking of modernising states. This is their determination to establish a separate identity unaligned to either West or East. The nationalist socialists insist that they are forging a new approach to economic development that avoids the errors and short-comings of both capitalism and communism.

The socialism of the Middle East has, in fact, been described as 'post-communistic', emerging as an alliance between the new middle class, the workers and the peasants, with the middle class clearly in charge.

In this connection it should be noted that all the socialist parties in the Middle East were founded later than the communist parties, and indeed, over the past two decades, communist parties in nearly every Arab country have been banned for far longer periods than they have been permitted to operate.

Socialism also has an important built-in advantage over communism in the Middle East in that its nationalist loyalty is not open to doubt.

10

Western European Socialism and Arab Socialism

It is clear from what has been said that whatever the exact nature of the socialism of the newly emerging states, it has been greatly influenced by marxism. However, it is also true that it owes a great deal to the socialism of Western Europe; and certain general comparisons can be made between the latter and the newer versions of socialism that have appeared in Asia, Africa and the Middle East since the Second World War.

Firstly, affinity between the two schools of thought is to be found in their common attitude towards capitalist free enterprise. Both regard this as synonymous with a minimal concern for the poor, unequal distribution of wealth and an undue influence exerted by the rich in the affairs of the people.

Nationalisation is generally regarded as an indispensable principle of socialism. But Arab Socialism has more in common with the pragmatic approach to nationalisation of Western Europe than with that of the extreme advocates of nationalisation as an article of socialist faith to be applied for doctrinaire reasons. The restraint, in fact, shown by Nasser in this matter, and the practical rather than theoretical reasons for embarking upon nationalisation when he did, have on occasion been a cause for dismay among marxist observers.

As for the relation of Arab Socialism to marxism, Nasser himself made some illuminating observations in a speech in Cairo in 1962.

He said: 'I have often said that our socialism is appropriate to our own circumstances. We do not copy the world's other social experiments; we study them without prejudice or chauvinism. But there are some basic differences between our socialism and marxist-leninist socialism.

'Marxist-leninism does not recognise religion; we acknowledge the existence of God and believe in religion.

'Marxist-leninism preaches the conversion of reactionary dictatorship into the dictatorship of the proletariat, which is the dictatorship of one class anyway. We, on the contrary, do not believe that dictatorship should pass from one class to another. This will breed civil war. We are converting a state of reactionary "bourgeois" dictatorship into one of the democracy of the whole people.

'Marxist-leninism advocates the violent eradication of the exploiting class. We, on the other hand, solve our problems without bloodshed. We give to this class, or rather to its members as individuals, the opportunity of a decent and honourable life.

'Marxist-leninism does not believe in private ownership. We distinguish between exploiting and non-exploiting private ownership. We are opposed only to the former but encourage the latter.

'Finally, Marxist-leninism stipulates the nationalisation of agricultural land. Our socialism does not. Rather, it believes in private ownership of agricultural land within the framework of a co-operative system.'

Nasser's socialism, although the outcome of a political revolution, has followed a gradual approach to the problems of socialisation. In this respect it is nearer to the fabianism of 'democratic socialism' than to the marxist-leninist concept of violent revolution. Other similarities of approach between Western fabianism and Arab Socialism in Egypt are their common belief in gradualism and the avoidance of violent clash between classes; and their view of the state as a social machine to be captured and used for the promotion of social welfare and social services, as the servant of the people rather than an instrument of domination.

For Nasser, man was the determining factor. The actual needs of man were justification for social change rather than any theoretical needs of the state or society. Although Nasser saw socialism, at least as far as Egypt and the Arab world were concerned, as inevitable, a sense of human values prevailed with him over Marx's theory of historical inevitability and over Stalin's concept of the inexorable march towards industrialisation. He would not countenance the concentration on heavy industries for the sake of the future if it meant sacrificing the well-being of the present generation with its already long history of suffering. Nor did he seek to eliminate the class structure suddenly and as an evil in itself. He believed in its gradual disappearance in the course of time.

Nasser's sense of the practical and his own countryside background affected his attitude to private property, leading him to believe in the role of a private sector in the economy, and particularly in the continuation of private ownership of agricultural land. This contrasts sharply with marxist thinking and is remote from stalinist practice in the 1930's. A somewhat similar situation exists today in Poland and Yugoslavia where between 85 and 90 per cent of the farm land is in private hands.

In Egypt, in addition to land, large apartment buildings may also be privately owned because this does not involve exploitation since there are high taxes on large incomes and the government controls rents.

For practising muslims such as Sadat and Algeria's

77

Boumedienne, the Quran constitutes a more authoritative and comprehensive scheme for the regulation of human society than does the Communist Manifesto or Das Kapital. Communism may offer certain organisational ideas of value to developing states, but Islam, as practised in its early days when, for example, important factors in the life of that time such as water and pasture were declared public property, is regarded by many muslims as the first 'socialist' society.

In an interesting correspondence in 1961 between Anwar Al-Sadat, then president of the U.A.R. National Assembly and Premier Khrushchev, Sadat wrote:

'The Arabs reject Western ideological concepts like capitalism, not because we hate them but because we believe they do not suit the nature, conditions, hopes, needs and requirements of our people.... This does not mean that communism, which proved successful in conditions prevailing in other countries, is suitable for successful application in our country. Our people refuse to be limited to this choice between capitalism and communism and believe that the ideological scope in the world extends further than this closed circle. They also believe they are capable of contributing creatively in adding to the richness of the world's ideology.'[1]

About this time, President Nasser stated: 'We have not permitted the establishment of a communist party in Egypt because we are sure that it can not act in conformity with its own will or work for the interest of the country. We are sure that it will receive inspiration from abroad and will work for foreigners. Communism in the U.A.R.,' he said, 'would mean that the country would have no will of its own, and we would follow the line of international communism and receive directions from it.'[2]

It is little wonder that two years after this a Western expert on Middle East affairs was to write: 'It is significant how little the Soviets have accomplished, in the way of injecting communism to the Arab bloodstream. Communism both as an ideology and as an organisation has failed to make appreciable headway among the Arabs in recent years. On balance, it has lost rather than gained ground.'[2]

Nasser believed that it was possible to resist an ideology only with another ideology. The democratic socialism of the West, however, has so far failed to convince the developing countries that it offered them either an alternative way to progress or an ideal to which they could respond. To them it seems to be applicable only to the most advanced areas of the world.

Suffering perhaps from its past relations with the underdeveloped world, Western capitalism, too, fails to put itself across. So the leadership of the newly established states is faced with a menacing ideological vacuum in addition to their formidable economic problems.

REFERENCES

[1] *The Egyptian Economic and Political Review* (Cairo, May-June, 1961), pp. 27-28.

[2] Charles Cremeans: *The Arabs and the World* (Praeger, New York, 1963), p. 294.

II

Soviet and Chinese Reactions to New Forms of 'Socialism'

In the early 1950's, communist ideologists began to use the term 'the national bourgeoisie' to describe the political élites in the newly independent countries which had led the struggle for freedom from Western domination. Obviously it was in the communist interest to support such movements as were anti-Western in the sense that they wished to terminate Western hegemony over their lands. Yet in almost all cases these movements were led by middle-class nationalists, not communists or men of working-class background.

Under Stalin, communism was not flexible enough to compromise with, and accommodate itself to such movements. One Soviet expert on Africa spoke of anti-colonialist movements, at this time, as being only concerned with taking advantage of the fruits of revolution and with seizing political power for the suppression and enslavement of the masses of the people. Nevertheless, he counselled that communism could use this special strategic stage of nationalist revolution. The nationalist group of officers led by Nasser who toppled King Farouk in 1952 and pressed for British evacuation of Egypt, were referred to by communist spokesmen at the time as 'a reactionary group'.

Since Khrushchev abandoned Stalin's two-camp anti-neutralist line, Soviet tactics have been to encourage the non-aligned, non-communist, Afro-Asian states, foreseeing that they would move towards 'the second revolution' and the eventual acceptance of communism. The Czechoslovak-Egyptian arms deal of 1955 coincided with this phase and Nasser was duly acclaimed by Russia as a nationalist, anti-imperialist hero.

Ideologically, this trend coincided with the enlargement by Khrushchev of the concept of a 'peaceful transition to socialism', originally formulated by Marx to apply to advanced parliamentary states. Now it was to include underdeveloped countries of Africa, Asia and Latin America, in a novel variant of the concept of 'continuous revolution'. According to this notion, progressive elements in a united front should seize power, adopt a hard line against the imperialists, restrict private capital within the country, and deprive the bourgeoisie of its economic and political positions, thus moving towards a national front under working-class leadership and ultimately 'a dictatorship' of the people.

This process was not to be, in the case of Egypt. By 1957 Nasser began advocating *Arab* socialism. And in 1958 a hastily arranged union with Syria was announced, upon Syria's request, to forestall a communist take-over. In December 1958 Nasser accused the Syrian communists of opposing the union with Egypt and attempting to subvert it after it had been formed.

Nasser was shocked to see Khrushchev take the defence of Arab communists, as if they were his responsibility, and there followed an exchange of politico-ideological attacks.

By the early 1960's, however, the Kremlin's evaluation of the political élites governing newly independent countries was beginning to shift again. Its line fell now somewhere between the indiscriminate castigations of the Stalin era and the recognition in these countries of the 'national bourgeoisie' of the early Khrushchev era.

By late 1960, after communist failures in Syria and Iraq, and disappointment in the development of relations with Egypt, the Soviets clearly embarked upon a major re-appraisal of their policies towards the new states of Africa and Asia. Part of the problem was a basic disagreement with the Chinese communists on policy towards these areas. The Soviets appeared to be in favour of a policy of coopera-tion with national revolutions, and of moving them along through various stages from that of preparation for social-ism to the final stage of communism—a continuation of the Khrushchev policy. The Chinese, on the other hand, were for violent revolution of the classic leninist type.

The new paternal note was struck at a dinner party in Moscow in 1961 given in honour of a visiting delegation from the U.A.R. National Assembly, when Mr Khrushchev addressed them in these words:

'You and we view matters differently. But this should not stand as a barrier between us. History will stand as judge. We are communists and you do not belong to this doctrine. Yet history will teach you.... We operate on a socialist basis. You, the Arabs, now understand this. But you do not understand the socialism which leads to com-munism. You are like a person learning the alphabet.... You are learning the "A". Socialism is the first letter in the alphabet which organises human society. While "B" is the beginning of communism. If you seek socialism you should not say you are against communism, since you place yourselves in an embarrassing situation and fall into the trap of imperialism.'

In striking contrast to Peking's silence at this period was the repeated Soviet praise of the socialist direction of cer-tain Egyptian developments in the fields of industrialisa-tion, and cooperative farming. The Soviet line was based on the then current Soviet theory that no matter how far removed from 'scientific' socialism local variants may be, closer relations with the communist world were a step in the right direction.

As the rivalry between the Soviet Union and China hardened, Peking's silence changed into a more active attitude, officials of the People's Republic of China, clinging to their conviction that only revolution internally and globally can usher in communism, began to make a different evaluation of the 'nationalist bourgeoisie' of the Afro-Asian countries on the non-capitalist path of development. The new Chinese view was that the newly independent states were now ready for revolution. It would have to be led by native communists and not by an alliance or partnership of 'nationalist bourgeoisie' and communists, as advocated by the Soviet Union.

Short of surrendering to communist leadership, the only way in which the nationalist bourgeoisies could find favour in Chinese eyes was by engaging in armed conflict with one of the imperialist powers, or by actively supporting liberation movements involved in such conflict.

Although, ideologically, both the Chinese and the Russians regarded the 'nationalist bourgeoisie' as an unreliable element in the anti-imperialist struggle, nevertheless, in practice both were, and still are, prepared to cooperate with governments led by 'bourgeois' nationalists—even when the latter refuse to recognise their native communists. The only condition is that these governments can in fact be useful in the primary conflict between the communist powers and the West. The difference is that the Russians judge this usefulness in terms of the support forthcoming to Russia's policies on peace, co-existence, disarmament and decolonisation in the United Nations and elsewhere, whereas the Chinese measure it more specifically in terms of militancy and readiness to engage in direct armed conflict with the 'imperialists' and to give active support to those so engaged.

The Soviets hope that the new 'socialist' leaders may not be able to solve their internal contradictions and that their conflicts with the European former colonial powers will make them more open to radical solutions. The hope is that with patience, the same conditions that the Chinese wish to create immediately will arise progressively out of the natural logic of events without undue risk or cost and without setbacks from premature initiatives such as the Kirkuk rising in Iraq in 1958.

Arab Socialism and Democracy

It now is necessary to examine to what extent Arab socialist policies in fact constitute a comprehensive, valid ideology.

From time to time Soviet writers such as Mayevsky, Potekhin, and Paloncy, derided Nasser's claim to be building socialism. Mayevsky objected particularly to the religious and spiritual basis for Arab Socialism and to its refusal to accept class conflict as inevitable. Potekhin stressed that there was no other way of building socialism than by the 'scientific' (leninist-marxist) method.

Although Khrushchev scoffed at the fact that Egyptians accepted socialism as a target but stopped short of recognising communism as their next logical goal, no specific attack was made on the acceptance of private ownership of up to one hundred acres of land and of housing property, nor upon the maintaining of the private sector in industry. This was presumably because it was all assumed to be part of an interim stage later to be left behind.

At the other end of the political spectrum there are those in the United States and elsewhere in the West, who see little difference between Arab Socialism and communism.

That such a misconception should exist today is probably not, in the main, the result of Russia's massive aid to the Arabs. This aid was accepted only after it had been previously, and in every case, asked for from the West and denied. It is rather the result of lack of information about

Arab life, culture and thought, coupled with twenty years of, perhaps understandable, effort by the supporters of Israel to portray the Arabs as friends of communism and thus as a menace to the West.

Those who fear that the line is narrow between an independent Arab nationalist and socialist state and one that is communist-controlled may be failing to assess the Islamic ideology that permeates Arab Socialism, and the strength this gives to its popular base—the Arab Socialist Union.

Nasser himself did not see Egypt as a fully socialist state. He saw it taking years to build the society of 'sufficiency and justice', but in the organisational structure he created he went a long way to prepare for such a society.

Egypt, despite its encouraging progress towards industrialisation and increased agricultural output up to the time of the disastrous Israeli war of 1967, has not yet reached a stage of self-sustained growth. The poverty of Egypt's villagers, who constitute the majority of the population, leaves the goal of equitable distribution of wealth far from realised.

Nevertheless, many would judge that, among all the non-communist socialist leaders of the new developing states—whether in Africa, Asia or Latin America—Nasser's policies have come nearest to what is generally thought of in the West as socialism.

If the promise of democracy is yet to be fulfilled in the Arab world, it is, to some extent, due to the fact that, almost as soon as they achieved freedom from colonial control, the Arabs were thrust into a continuous state of defensive war with Israel; and have been compelled to subordinate their economic and cultural development to the demands of self-defence.

However, the commitment remains to achieve democracy and much of the groundwork has now been laid. Much will depend on leadership that inspires the people's vision. Much depends upon the training of a generation of 'new men' for a new society. Much also depends upon the response of the people themselves and upon their ability to adapt to a world of modern techniques.

In the final resort the outcome will depend upon the strength of individual determination to bring about a just and free society. For no people can be governed democratically unless and until they want to participate and have earned their right to do so by their sense of responsibility.

Part Three

The National Charter

Submitted by President Nasser

to the National Congress of the U.A.R.

21 May 1962

A new and abridged translation

1. THE 1952 REVOLUTION

On 23 July 1952 began a new and important stage in the history of the long struggle of the Arab people in Egypt.

On that memorable day the people embarked upon a revolutionary experiment fraught with difficulties and danger.

Their genuine and sustained belief in the revolution has already made possible a basic change in their way of life and brought the realisation of many of their greatest human hopes within grasp.

The greatness of the change the Egyptian people achieved can only be appreciated if seen against the background of the powers that lurked in ambush to nip in the bud every branch of hope before it grew.

Foreign invaders were in occupation on its territory. Nearby were armed military bases to awe the Egyptian people and suppress resistance.

The alien royal family had been ruling according to its whims and fancies and accepting national humiliation and servility.

The feudal landlords possessed the fields and monopolised their crops, leaving nothing to the millions of toiling fellaheen except the straw left after the harvest.

Capitalists exploited Egyptian wealth, dominating the government and making it serve their interests.

The revolution appears the more remarkable when we recall that it began its revolutionary march with no political organisation to face the problems of the battle. Moreover, this march started without a recognised theory for revolutionary change.

In those eventful days the basis of work was the famous 'six principles' which summarised the aims of the people's struggle:

The first was to end imperialism, represented by the

British military occupation of the Canal Zone and its Egyptian agents.

The second was to end the system of feudal landlords.

The third was to end the domination of capital over the government.

The fourth was the establishment of a basis of social justice.

The fifth was to build a powerful national army.

The sixth was to establish a sound democratic system.

The success of the revolution owed much to five characteristics which permeated it.

The first was a will for revolutionary change which rejected all the old restrictions and limitations on the rights of the masses.

The second was the concept of a revolutionary vanguard to act in the interests of the people.

The third was a profound sense of history together with a belief in man's ability to influence it.

The fourth was an openness of mind to experience elsewhere in the world and a readiness to benefit from it, while avoiding extremism.

The fifth was unshakable faith in God, the Prophets and the sacred messages which He passed on to humanity in all places and at all times, as a guide to justice and righteousness.

2. THE NECESSITY OF THE REVOLUTION

Experience has shown, and continues to confirm, that the only course which the Arab world can take to head for a better future is a revolutionary one.

It is the only means by which the Arab nation can free itself of its shackles, and rid itself of the dark heritage which has burdened it.

Revolutionary change is the only way to overcome under-development, forced on the Arab nation through years of suppression and exploitation. Conventional methods of work are no longer capable of bridging the gap in development which exists between the Arab nation and advanced countries.

It is therefore imperative to deal radically with matters and to ensure the mobilisation of all the nation's material and spiritual potentialities to undertake this responsibility.

Moreover, revolutionary change is the only way to face the challenge offered by the astounding scientific discoveries, which at present help widen the gap of development between one country and another. With the knowledge they reveal, these discoveries add to the progress of advanced countries and, in so doing, widen the gap further between them and others, despite all the efforts the latter may exert to narrow it.

The revolutionary path is the only bridge which the Arab nation can cross to reach the future to which it aspires.

The Arab revolution needs to develop in three ways if it is to win the battle of destiny it is now fighting:

First, it needs an ideology based on rational conviction, enlightened thought and matured in free discussion, free from extremist and terrorist pressures.

Secondly, it needs flexibility to the changing circumstances without sacrificing the objectives and the moral ideals of the struggle.

Thirdly, it needs clarity of objective, which is never swept away by emotion and diverted from the high road of the national struggle.

The objectives of the Arab struggle are:

Freedom, Socialism and Unity.

Freedom means independence for the country and freedom for the citizen.

Socialism is both a means and an end. Its end being sufficiency and justice for every citizen.

Unity is the natural order of a nation.

The quest for a new road is not prompted merely by a desire for innovation or for considerations of national dignity. It arises from the fact that the Arab nation is now facing new circumstances, demanding new solutions.

The outstanding changes that took place in the world after the Second World War may be summed up as follows:

First: The spectacular strengthening of the nationalist movements in Asia, Africa and Latin America to the extent that they have now become an internationally potent force.

Second: The emergence of the communist camp as an enormous power, with steadily increasing material and moral weight and effectiveness in confronting the capitalist camp.

Third: The great scientific and technological advance opening up unlimited horizons for development.

The same advance was also achieved in the development of arms which are now potentially so destructive to all parties involved that they themselves have become a deterrent against war.

The same scientific and technological progress has taken place in the means of communications, as a result of which distances and barriers both physical and intellectual between one country and another have now virtually disappeared.

Fourth: In the field of international relations, there has been an increasing weight of moral pressure such as that exercised by the United Nations, the non-aligned states and world public opinion.

In this changed situation imperialism has had to resort to indirect methods such as the formation of economic blocs, the waging of cold war, and attempts to undermine the confidence of the smaller nations in their capacity to develop themselves and to provide an equal and positive contribution to the service of human society.

While the aims of the Arab national struggle remain freedom, socialism, and unity, world conditions have often influenced the means of achievement.

It is no longer believed that freedom can be attained by placating the imperialists or bargaining with them. In 1956 the Arab people in Egypt were able to take up arms and defend their freedom, achieving a memorable victory in Port Said. In the same way in their determination to secure freedom, the Arab people carried on a war in Algeria, lasting more than seven years.

Moreover, socialist action is no longer compelled to follow literally principles formulated in the nineteenth century.

The progress in means of production, the development of nationalist and labour movements, the increasing demand for world peace, as a result of the influence of moral forces and, at the same time of the effect of the balance of atomic terror—all these factors combine to create a new situation for socialist experiments—entirely different from what existed in the past.

In facing this world the Arab revolution must have a new approach that does not shut itself up within the confines of theories which are at once limited and limiting, yet does not deny itself access to the rich storehouse of experience gained by other striving peoples in their similar struggles.

The torch of civilisation has passed from one hand to another, but in each land it crossed, it acquired a fresh supply of oil to make the flame burn brighter.

Social experiences are capable of passing from one place to another but not of being blindly copied; they are capable of useful study and examination, but not of being learnt by rote.

3. THE ROOTS OF THE EGYPTIAN STRUGGLE

Originally there were no barriers dividing the Arab nation's homeland. It stood exposed to the same currents of history.

Egypt in particular had close links with the surrounding area. It consciously, and sometimes unconsciously, influenced it and was in turn influenced by it as a part interacts with the whole. This is borne out by the study of the Pharaonic civilisation and again by events during the Greek and Roman periods.

The Islamic conquest brought a new unity of spiritual thought and sentiment. Under Islam, the Egyptian people, guided by the message of Mohammed, assumed a major role in the defence of civilisation. Before the whole area was swept by the darkness of the Ottoman invasion, the Egyptian people had assumed leadership in the interest of the whole region.

The Egyptian people bore the brunt of repelling the first wave of European colonialism, masquerading behind the Cross of Jesus—although, in fact, colonialism and the message of that great teacher are poles apart.

The Egyptian people also bore the brunt of repelling the attacks of the Tartars who swept over the plains of the East and crossed its mountains bringing destruction and ruin.

The Egyptian people also bore the moral responsibility of preserving the rich heritage of Arab civilisation. They made their Al-Azhar university a stronghold of resistance against the weakness and disintegration imposed by the Ottoman Caliphate in the name of religion.

It was not the French campaign against Egypt that led to the Egyptian awakening at the beginning of the nineteenth century as some historians claim. For when the French came they found Al-Azhar simmering with new life. The French campaign also found the Egyptian people resentful of Ottoman colonialism disguised as the Caliphate, which imposed on them a false conflict between genuine religious faith and their will to live as free people.

The French campaign, however, did bring a new revolutionary stimulus to the Egyptian people at that time.

It brought glimpses of modern science developed by Europe out of the scientific knowledge taken over from earlier civilisations, among them the Pharaonic and Arab civilisations.

Furthermore, it brought outstanding professors who studied the affairs of Egypt and uncovered the secrets of its ancient history.

This stimulus inspired self-confidence and opened up new horizons before the eager imagination of the Egyptian people.

This popular awakening was the driving force behind the reign of Mohammed Ali. It is almost universally assumed that Mohammed Ali laid the foundation of modern Egypt. Yet the tragedy was that he saw the popular movement only as a springboard for his ambitions, and he took Egypt into futile adventures which were not in the true interests of the people.

While modern Japan, whose awakening started about the same time as that of Egypt, proceeded steadily, the adventures of Egypt's rulers opened the gates to foreign interference; and unfortunately this setback occurred at a stage of colonialism when it had developed from mere occupation of colonies and the draining of their resources to a stage of re-investment of the capital created from those colonies.

International financial monopolies started to play their dangerous role in Egypt. They channelled their activities in two directions, namely the digging of the Suez Canal and the transformation of Egypt into a vast plantation. The aim was to provide British industry with the cotton which America rarely exported to her after the end of British domination in America. Later, American cotton was withheld entirely from Britain as a result of the American Civil War.

During that period, Egypt lived through a dreadful experience. All her resources were spent in the interests of foreign powers and foreign adventurers who succeeded in getting the Khedives of the Mohammed Ali dynasty under their power. Yet the spirit of the people was never broken.

Thousands of Egyptian youths were sent to Europe to master modern science in the reign of Mohammed Ali. Returning home, these youths brought good seeds which the fertile revolutionary soil of Egypt welcomed and nursed to produce a flourishing culture on the banks of the Nile.

Britain in particular, because of her concern about the route to India, never lost sight of Egypt and threw all her weight against the revolutionary popular tide which began to rise against the alien Mohammed Ali dynasty, and which reached a peak in the Orabi revolution.

The British military occupation of Egypt in 1882 was an expression of the determination of colonialism to guarantee foreign financial interests and to support the authority of the Khedive against the people.

Hardly had the din of the guns which bombed Alexandria, and the noise of the battle of Tel-el-Kebir faded, when new voices were heard, voices expressing the awakening which difficulties and disasters could not silence.

Ahmed Orabi's voice was stopped but that of Mustafa Kamel began to ring out loudly in Egypt.

This period, which the imperialists and those who collaborated with them thought to be a period of stagnation, was one of the richest periods in the history of Egypt in its soul-searching and its mustering anew of revolutionary effort.

During this period, Mohammed Abdu's call for religious reform was heard, and Lutfi El Sayed proclaimed that Egypt should belong to the Egyptians. Qasim Amin, at the same time, was calling for the emancipation of women.

Saad Zaghlul led the 1919 Revolution. There are three reasons for its failure.

First, the revolutionary leadership almost completely overlooked the demand for social change. It failed to see that a revolution cannot achieve its aims for the people unless its drive goes beyond the political façade, reflected in the demand for independence, and tackles the core of the economic and social problem.

Secondly, the revolutionary leadership at the time failed to extend their vision beyond Sinai and, learning from history, to appreciate the connection between Egyptian patriotism and Arab nationalism. It also failed to learn from the enemy they fought, who had a united plan for the entire Arab nation. And it failed to see the danger of the Balfour Declaration which set up Israel as a dividing line across the Arab territory, and as a threatening bridgehead.

At this time, the Arab nation suffered such humiliation that imperialist agents were even able to take over the Arab revolutionary movement, and thrones were set up for those who betrayed the Arab struggle and deviated from its aims. In the meantime the national revolutionary movement in Egypt imagined that these developments did not concern it.

Thirdly, the revolutionary leadership did not adapt its methods of struggle to the methods adopted by its opposition. Imperialism discovered that military force only fanned the flames of popular revolution; and so the sword was replaced by deceit. Formal and superficial concessions were made which failed to distinguish between appearances and reality.

Independence was granted only in form. The slogan of freedom was proclaimed while its reality was kept back.

Thus the struggle ended by accepting an independence of no content; a sham freedom under the guns of occupation.

The 1936 treaty, concluded between Egypt and Britain, and signed by a national front that comprised all the political parties active at the time, was like a document of surrender to the great bluff by which the 1919 Revolution was taken in. The preamble to the treaty stipulated that Egypt was independent, while every clause deprived this independence of all value or significance.

4. THE INTER-WAR SETBACK

The really dangerous period in the long struggle of the Egyptian people was that following the setback in 1919. But, in the event, it provided the psychological preparation for the July 1952 Revolution. This period, had it not been for the adamant will and true mettle of the people, could have led the country to a state of despair, stifling and paralysing every incentive for change.

It was a period of misleading façades concealing the shaky nature of the 1919 Revolution.

The former leadership of the revolution was still in the forefront but it had lost all its revolutionary fire. It had surrendered all the demands raised by the people in 1919 to the big landlords who became the backers of the party organisations.

A group of intellectuals emerged in this corrupt party atmosphere. These could have safeguarded the aspirations of the genuine revolution, but temptation was stronger than resistance.

Their deviation paved the way for a batch of capitalists who took on the role of the nineteenth-century foreign adventurers, disregarding the true needs of the country. These people only cared for the exploitation of the country's wealth in the shortest time possible.

Sometimes these elements were sponsored by the palace, sometimes by imperialism. They had one and the same interest and stood in one camp. Superficial differences may have arisen between them at times, but the major factor that they had in common was their opposition to the people's interests and the trend of progress. The power of the people constituted a menace to their position.

At the same time there was a democratic façade which was used to divert the people from their rightful demands. Democracy, as it was exercised in Egypt, during this period, was a shameful farce.

The voice of the people was steered according to the will of the ruling powers and their collaborators. That was the natural result of neglecting the social aspect of the 1919 Revolution. For those who controlled the means of live-lihood of the peasants and workers controlled their votes.

The constitution accepted by the revolutionary leader-ship as a gift from the intruder became a mere scrap of paper giving only lip-service to the rights of the people.

The leadership of the popular struggle had surrendered before the mounting power of the palace. They all knelt down seeking the favours that would lead to the seats of power. They abandoned the people and lost all self-respect. They sold their souls to the devil, reaching a point where a change of cabinet could be effected by payment of a certain price to the palace.

When national leadership uproots itself from the people's soul then it condemns itself to death.

The Motherland will feel for a long time the bitter humiliation it experienced at that period when the imperialists made light of its struggle. The bitter hatred felt by our people towards imperialism, which they still experience despite the lapse of time, emanates from this period.

Imperialism, at that time, not only intimidated all the peoples of the Arab nation but also made light of their struggle for the right to a decent life.

Imperialism denied all the pledges it made during the First World War. The Arab nation was then given the impression that the day of independence and unity was near. Its hopes were dashed. The Arab states were divided among the imperialist states to satisfy their ambitions. Moreover, the imperialist statesmen coined humiliating words such as 'mandate' and 'trusteeship' to cover up their schemes.

Part of the Arab territory, Palestine, was handed to an aggressive racial movement to be used by the imperialists as a whip in their hands to hold down the Arabs should they ever be able to renew their struggles.

The imperialists intended this territory to be a barrier dividing the Arab East from the Arab West, and a constant drain on the energy of the Arab nation diverting it from positive constructive tasks.

It was ironical that Arab troops which entered Palestine in 1917 to recover Arab rights should be under the supreme command of a British officer who received his orders from the very statesman who was soon to give the Zionist movement the Balfour Declaration on which the Jewish state in Palestine was based.

Long years will elapse before the Arab nation can forget the bitterness of the experience it underwent during that period. The Arab nation emerged from that experience with an adamant determination to defeat imperialism.

The Egyptian people were ready to resume their struggle even before the end of the Second World War and before the occupying tanks had gone from their main cities.

They expressed themselves through an obstinate refusal to take part in the war which to them was but a strife over colonies and markets between racialist Nazism and Anglo-French imperialism, which was involving mankind in tremendous tragedies, and the people as a whole were not behind those who collaborated with the occupying power, seeking the black market profits of wartime.

This was a preparatory stage, a period of indignation which paved the way for the revolution. Anger is a passive phase. Revolution is a positive action aiming at the establishment of new systems.

The anger of the Egyptian people which paved the way for change was no longer confined to a few individuals; it spread among the entire people. The burning of Cairo, in January 1952, could have been stopped had it not been for the outburst of anger by the people which fanned its flames. The dominant ruling class in the capital was unaware of the feelings of the people, so deeply were they immersed in their luxuries. But the spark of anger caused more fires in Cairo at that time than all the foreign agents.

The greatest thing about the revolution of 23 July 1952 was that the armed forces, which set the stage for it, were not its instigators but were the tool of the popular will.

The great achievement of the revolutionary vanguard in the army on that immortal night was the take-over of the army and the placing of it in its rightful place, namely at the service of the people.

This meant that the popular struggle was provided with the necessary arms to enable it to face the forces of occupation and to repel counter action.

The revolution itself did not take place on the night of 23 July. But on that glorious night the gate was flung open for it.

The great event which occurred on the eve of 23 July

could have ended merely in a change of cabinet. Or, on the other hand, it could have turned into a military dictatorship to add one more to the list of fascist experiments. But the genuine strength of the revolutionary concept steered the course of events and enlisted all nationalist elements in the struggle.

The needs of our country were such that it was not enough to patch up the old decaying building, to try to keep it from falling by means of supports and to give the exterior a fresh coat of paint. What was needed was a new and strong building resting on firm foundations and towering high in the sky.

The most powerful argument against the reasoning of those who called for moderate reform was that the old building did actually crumble and fall to pieces when faced with the new situation.

The sudden and complete collapse of the system that had existed before the revolution underlined the futility of any attempt to patch it up.

Yet the bringing down of the old régime was not the main objective of the revolutionary movement. It was more concerned with the setting up of a new building rather than with the ruins.

The gate which was flung open on the eve of 23 July remained open for a considerable period of time before the inevitable and long awaited change made its appearance.

This was, in the first place, because the ruins of the old régime cluttered the way. There were still around the remnants of its out-dated cupidity. Also the revolutionary vanguard that was responsible for the events on the eve of 23 July was not entirely ready to assume the responsibility of carrying through the revolutionary change for which it had paved the way.

It opened the gate before the revolution under the banner of the famous 'six principles' but these principles were only banners for the revolution and not a technique for revolutionary action or a method to bring about the radical changes needed.

5. ASPECTS OF TRUE DEMOCRACY

The essence of a revolution is popular and progressive action. It is the action of a people determined to remove the obstacles and barriers to a better way of life, as they conceive of it.

A revolution is not the work of one individual, nor of one group. The validity of a revolution lies in its degree of popularity. Also in the extent to which it is an expression of the will of the masses, and in the extent to which it mobilises them to rebuild the future.

Revolution, also, signifies progress. The masses do not call for change merely for its own sake. They do so in order to attain a better life. Material and social under-development are the real driving force behind the will to change and behind the thrust from what actually is, to what should, and could be.

A democratic spirit is the mark of a revolution that has genuine popular backing.

Democracy means the assertion of the sovereignty of the people, the placing of all authority in their hands and the consecration of power to serve their ends. Similarly, a socialist spirit marks the progressive nature of a revolution.

Socialism means the setting up of a society on a basis of sufficiency and justice for all, of work and equal opportunity for all, and of planned production and services.

Both democracy and socialism could be said to be revolutionary concepts.

Democracy is political freedom while socialism is social freedom. The two cannot be separated since they are both indispensable to true freedom. They are, so to speak, its two wings without either of which it cannot soar to the horizons of the future.

In the midst of their victory in the battle of Suez, the Egyptian people realised that it was not, this time, their freedom that they had won. Rather the battle had enabled them to discover their abilities and potentialities and to release their will to shape their freedom in accordance with the principles of the revolution.

The question which arose quite naturally in the aftermath of the victory at Suez was the following: 'To whom does this determination to be free, which the Egyptian people emerged with from the terrible battle, really belong?'

The only answer was: 'It belongs to the whole people, and it can serve no other cause but theirs.' A people does not wrench its will from the clutches of usurpers to lay it aside in the museums of history, but to make it a power harnessed to the meeting of its needs.

This stage is the most dangerous in the history of nations. It is the point at which many popular movements have suffered a setback, when at first they seemed full of hope. For after the first victory over external pressure they have forgotten themselves. They have wrongly assumed that their revolutionary aims had all been realised, forgetting that internal elements of exploitation are always closely linked with the forces of external pressure.

Later such popular movements discover, often too late, that in their failure to bring about economic change, they have robbed political freedom of its validity. Similarly, at this critical stage other popular movements run into trouble when, in their internal changes, they follow doctrinaire policies unrelated to actual national conditions.

Real solutions to the problems of one people cannot be imported ready-made from the experiences of another. This is not to reject all the solutions reached by others. For nations pass through a stage akin to adolescence, during which they need all the intellectual sustenance they can get hold of. But they also need to digest this food and mix with it all the secretions produced by their own living cells.

It is true that a nation at this stage needs to know all that goes on around it. Yet what it primarily needs is to find its own life on its own soil.

In the life of a nation, as in the life of an individual, the way to maturity and clarity of vision is through trial and error, and democracy is not achieved by copying the formal constitutional façades of others.

After the 1919 popular movement Egypt accepted the deceit of a sham democracy. After the first recognition of Egypt's independence by imperialism, in 1931, the revolutionary leadership surrendered to pseudo-democracy with a constitutional façade that had no real content.

As a result imperialism gave no weight to the word 'independence' written on paper and did not hesitate to tear it up at any time that suited its interests.

The façade of democracy only represented the reactionaries who were not prepared to break off relations with imperialism or stop collaborating with it. Therefore it was logical to find that the cabinets under the democracy of reaction and under the so-called national independence could only function at the behest of the official representative of imperialism in Egypt. At times, these governments were formed according to his instructions. At one stage a government was brought into power by imperialist tanks.

If feudalism is the economic system prevailing in a country, inevitably the political freedom therein can only be the freedom of feudalism; and a parliament established by a constitution that does not safeguard the interests of the people inevitably protects the interests of those who bestowed the constitution.

Undoubtedly some voices were raised within parliament calling for the rights of the people. But these appeals came to nothing. Actually it was not unhelpful for the representatives of reaction to have an outlet for popular indignation so long as it was in possession of all the safety-valves.

The freedom of the vote without the freedom of earning a living lost all its value and was a deception of the people.

Under these circumstances the right to vote meant three things.

Firstly, in the villages where voting was compulsory for the peasant, he had no alternative but to cast his vote in favour of, or according to the wishes of the owner of the land. Otherwise he had to bear the consequences and be expelled from the land where he worked and earned his subsistence.

In addition, in both villages and cities, the buying of votes enabled those with the capital to guarantee the election of its nominees.

Furthermore, the ruling elements did not hesitate, on occasion, to resort to open forgery if they felt the results conflicted with their interests.

The conditions governing the polling system, in particular, the excessively large monetary deposit, discouraged the worker from even approaching the game of polling, for such it was.

At the same time, the ignorance of the people made the secrecy of polling, which is the primary guarantee to its freedom, virtually impossible.

Political organisation, the backbone of popular representation, was also under these circumstances ineffective.

Millions of peasants, even the small landowners, were not allowed to organise themselves in cooperatives to enable them to protect the output of their land and make their voices heard even locally, let alone in ruling circles in the capital.

Millions of agricultural labourers lived in conditions akin to forced labour, with wages near to starvation level. They worked with no security for the future. Thousands of workers employed in industry and trade were also unable to challenge the will of the ruling caste. The trade union movement, which gave leadership to the workers, encountered great difficulties, among them attempts to corrupt it.

During that period, there was no freedom of criticism nor freedom of the press, and technical developments in printing made newspaper publishing a complicated capitalist operation.

In the field of education, which might otherwise have released new energies of hope, the rulers sought to make sure that only those concepts which expressed their interests were taught and this was reflected in the system and methods of education.

Successive generations of Egyptian youth were taught that their country was neither suitable for nor capable of industrialisation. In their text books they read their national history in distorted versions. Their national heroes were described as lost in a mist of doubt and uncertainty while those who had betrayed the nation were glorified and venerated.

Successive generations of Egyptian youth attended schools and universities whose educational programmes aimed at nothing more than to turn out civil servants to work for the existing system and under laws and regulations which disregarded the interests of the people.

Out of this revolutionary situation which the Egyptian people were determined to change, and to change in a democratic way, the following formula for action evolved:

First, political democracy could not be separated from social democracy. No citizen could be regarded as free to vote unless he was free from exploitation and his mind free from anxiety and insecurity.

Secondly, political democracy could not exist under the domination of any one class. Democracy meant the authority and sovereignty of the entire people.

The inevitable and natural class struggles could not be ignored but their resolution could be arrived at peacefully and with the aim of creating national and class unity.

The collaboration between the forces of reaction and capital had to be ended. The road could then be opened for democratic interaction between the various component elements of the nation, namely the farmers, workers, soldiers, intellectuals and capital.

In the third place, the unity created by the cooperation between those national elements should take concrete form in the Arab Socialist Union. This union will be the authority representing the people and will provide the driving force behind the revolution. It will also be the guardian of the people's rights.

In view of the enormous powers vested in the Arab Socialist Union the new constitution of the United Arab Republic must make sure that its popular organisations based on free elections fairly represent the majority of the population.

For this reason the new constitution will ensure that the farmers and workers will get half the seats in the popular organisations at all levels, including the House of Representatives.

The authority of the elected popular councils of the Arab Socialist Union will be raised above that of the executive machinery of the state; so that the people will always be the leaders of national action. This will also ensure the revolutionary drive against the dead hand of the administrative machinery. Again, local government will gradually take over some of the authority of the state on behalf of the people, who are in a good position to assess their own problems and find the proper solutions.

Within the framework of the Arab Socialist Union, elements fit for leadership will be recruited and collective leadership developed which can guard against individual irresponsibility and ensure the reign of democracy.

Fourthly, popular organisations, especially cooperatives and trade unions, need to play an effective and influential role in promoting sound democracy. These organisations should form an advance guard in the various fields of democratic action.

Fifthly, free criticism and self-criticism are important safeguards of freedom.

The ownership of the press by the people was achieved by the law of press organisation which ensured independence both of reactionary forces and of the government machinery. This law acquired for the people a most valuable medium for free expression of opinion and for criticism.

Finally, the new conception of democracy inherent in the revolution must intimately affect the life of the individual citizen.

The object of education is no longer to turn out employees to work in government offices. The educational curriculum must be re-designed to enable the individual to reshape his life. Laws also must be redrafted to apply to the new social structure. Moreover, justice, which is the sacred right of every individual, should never be an expensive commodity, beyond the reach of the citizen. Justice should be accessible to every individual without financial obstacles or administrative complications.

The government statutes have to be radically changed, since most of them were drawn up to serve but one class. They have to be transformed to uphold the democratic rights of all the people.

Democratic action in these fields will make possible the

development of a new culture with new values. Such a culture will be profoundly aware of the human being and sincere in expressing his thought and feeling. It will inspire the creative energies latent in him towards the building of a truly democratic society.

6. THE SOCIALIST SOLUTION

Socialism is the way to social freedom. Social freedom requires that an opportunity be provided for every citizen to obtain a fair share of the national wealth. Whether or not socialism offered a solution to the problem of under-development in Egypt was never open to question. The socialist solution was historically inevitable, imposed by the realities of the situation, by the popular mood and by the changing trend of world opinion in the second part of the twentieth century.

The achievements of capitalism were identified with imperialism. The countries of the capitalist world built their economic thrust on the basis of the investments they made in their colonies. The wealth of India produced the British capital which was used in the development of agriculture and industry in Britain.

Britain depended much upon the Lancashire textile industry and the transformation of Egypt into a large cotton-plantation made her into an artery pumping blood into the heart of Britain's economy. The cost was of course borne by the starving Egyptian fellah.

Gone is the day of imperialist pillage, when the wealth of countries was looted to serve the interests of outsiders over whom there was no legal or moral control.

On the other hand, there have been systems of progress which realised their objectives at the expense of the working people, by a ruthless application of ideology which sacrificed the lives of whole generations for the sake of others yet unborn.

The nature of the age no longer allows of such things. Progress through exploitation or through the forced labour system is no longer compatible with the human values of today.

Those who call for freedom for capital imagining that to be the high-road to progress are gravely mistaken.

In the underdeveloped countries capital is no longer able to lead the economic drive. The powerful world monopolies leave only two ways open for capitalism in the countries aspiring to progress. Either it must depend upon government subsidies paid for by the masses; or it must relate itself to the world monopolies, thus turning itself into their appendage.

Plans aimed at expanding the base of national wealth can never be left to the haphazard ways of private capital with its unpredictable ways. The fair distribution of the national effort can never be accomplished through voluntary efforts, however well-intentioned. The people must control the tools of production and the distribution of the national product. This is the socialist solution and the way to democracy in all its social and political forms.

Control over the tools of production does not necessitate the nationalisation of all the means of production; neither does it mean the abolition of private ownership or any infringement on the legitimate right of inheritance. But it does mean the creation of a public sector that would lead progress in all fields and bear the main responsibility for development.

The socialist solution enables all elements in the process of production to unite their energies to rebuild society on the basis of a carefully studied and comprehensive plan.

Efficient socialist planning is the only method which guarantees the use of all national resources in a practical, scientific and humane way for the common good and prosperity of the masses.

It is not only a process of working out the possible, it is a process of tackling the seemingly impossible and giving the people hope.

Great strides have been taken in enabling the public sector to give a lead to the nation. In the field of communications and services, it is intended that the railways, roads, ports, airports, dams, and other public services should come within the framework of public ownership.

In the field of industry, the majority of the heavy, medium and mining industries will be nationalised but light industries will be left open to private ownership, with the public sector playing a guiding role that ensures the people's interests are protected.

Although overseas trade will be under state control, private capital will be encouraged to participate in the export trade, while the public sector keeps a major share in order to preclude possible fraudulency. If a percentage could be defined in that field, the public sector must be in charge of three quarters of all exports while the private sector has the remaining share.

As for internal trade, the public sector will be in charge of at least one quarter of this to prevent monopoly and expand the range of activities.

In the field of finance, banks will be publicly owned; and in the field of real-estate there will be a clear difference between two kinds of private ownership: that which opens the gates to exploitation, and non-exploiting ownership which does its share in the service of the national economy while serving at the same time the interests of the owners themselves.

In the field of ownership of rural land, the agrarian reform laws have limited individual ownership to one hundred feddans, and the spirit of the law implies that this limitation should cover the whole family, namely: father, mother and children under age, otherwise the combining of family ownerships could create again feudalised estates.

As regards ownership of buildings, the laws of taxation on buildings and the laws limiting rents place ownership of buildings beyond the reach of exploitation. Yet constant supervision is imperative, although the increase in the publicly-owned and co-operative housing will help, in a practical manner, to combat attempts at exploitation in this field.

It is of prime importance that our nationalisation be freed from the stigmas that private interests have tried to attach to it.

Nationalisation is but the transfer of certain of the means of production from the sphere of private ownership to that of public ownership. It does not diminish individual initiative, as alleged by the enemies of socialism, but rather inspires public interest.

Some mistakes may occur during this process of evolution, but we must remember that the new hands that have assumed the responsibility are in need of training and it is inevitable that there should be some temporary difficulties.

Nationalisation is not, as advocated by some, a punishment inflicted upon private capital. The transfer of the means of production from the sphere of private ownership to that of public ownership is more significant than this. The private sector has its effective role in the development plan and must be protected to fulfil that part.

The private sector is now required to renovate itself and strike a new path of creative effort not dependent, as in the past, on excessive profiteering.

Progress through socialism is a consolidation of the bases of sound democracy, the democracy of all the people. The socialist path, providing opportunities for a peaceful settlement of the class struggle and affording possibilities for dissolving class distinctions, opens the way to equality of opportunity for all.

Socialism and democracy form the wings of freedom with which mankind can soar to the distant horizons of its aspirations.

7. SOCIETY AND THE BATTLE FOR PRODUCTION

Gone is the day when the destiny of the people of the Arab nation was decided in foreign capitals, at the tables of international conferences and in palaces allied with imperialism. The Arab recovered his right to fashion his own life through the revolution, and it will be in meeting the challenge of the battle of production that he will establish the place he merits under the sun.

Production is the criterion by which the dynamism of the Arab will be judged. By production we can end our underdevelopment and speed up progress.

The objective of the revolution to double national income at least once every ten years is not a mere slogan. It is the calculated assessment of the effort required to tackle underdevelopment keeping in mind the population.

The population increase is the most ominous problem facing the Egyptian people in its drive to raise the standard of living effectively. While the attempts at family-planning deserve every support, a drive to increase production is still the basic need.

The doubling of the national income every ten years would mean a rate of economic development greatly exceeding the rate of increase in the population. The attainment of this goal is possible without sacrificing today's citizens for the sake of those still to be born.

To attain this goal, it is not necessary to exhaust the

people's energies. All that it requires is honest and systematic work inspired by the vision of setting up a new society with new moral values, and with exciting prospects for mankind.

It will require colossal efforts in the fields of agriculture and industry and in the framework that supports the economy, particularly transport.

The Arab application of socialism does not involve nationalising the land. From experience and study it believes in individual ownership of land, within limits that would not permit of monopoly control.

This conclusion is not just a response to the sentimental longing of farmers for the ownership of land, but it derives from the actual conditions of agriculture in Egypt, and recognises particularly the capacity of the Egyptian 'fellah' for creative work, given the right conditions.

Moreover, long ago Egyptian agriculture adopted a sound socialist approach to its most complicated problems, such as those of irrigation and drainage, which have been for a long time within the framework of public ownership. The solution to the problems of agriculture does not, however, lie in transferring land into public ownership. It lies in individual ownership of land, and the provision of the right of ownership to the largest number of wage-earners, together with support from agricultural co-operatives.

Agricultural co-operation is much more than mere provision of credit. It includes the pooling of agricultural machinery and know-how. It goes parallel with the financial process which protects the 'fellah' and liberates him from moneylenders and middlemen who used to take the largest part of the fruit of his labour. Co-operation also helps the farmer in marketing.

The solution to the problem of the land in Egypt is to increase the number of landowners. Such was the aim of the laws of land-reform issued in 1952 and 1961 and this, together with the raising of production, was the motive behind the great irrigation projects associated with the Aswan High Dam. This dam has become the symbol of the will and determination of the people to fashion their own life. It also symbolises the determination to provide land-ownership for multitudes of 'fellaheen' for whom this opportunity was never provided throughout centuries of continuous feudal rule.

The success of this attempt at solving the agricultural problem by increasing the number of landowners depends upon relating the economy to the small land-holder.

In addition, agriculture must be extended horizontally by reclaiming the desert. The processes of land reclamation must never cease for a second. The area of green fields must become larger every day in the Nile Valley. We should reach a stage at which every drop of the Nile water can be transformed on its banks into creative life, for today many are waiting for their turn to own land in their country.

Agriculture must also be extended vertically through raising the productivity of cultivated land. Modern chemistry has touched in a revolutionary way the methods of cultivation. Moreover, wonderful scientific possibilities enable us to develop the animal wealth of the farmer. There are also big possibilities in scientific variation of agricultural crops.

Industrialisation opens vast scope for employment in the countryside. We should remember this at a time when we believe that the right to work is a vital human right.

Industrialisation will also help change the face of life in the villages in a revolutionary way; and the village needs to reach a civilised level. This is not only demanded by justice, it is also a fundamental requirement of development.

The town has a moral responsibility towards the village.

It has to undertake serious work in the village without any feeling of superiority.

When the village reaches the civilised standard of the town particularly in the field of culture, the villagers' capacity for planning will start. This will affect the population problem.

Ability to appreciate the necessity of planning in life is the basic solution to the problem of the continuous increase of the population. This maturity will change the individual's feeling of submission to fate and replace it with a feeling of responsibility that will drive him to plan the family economy.

Our approach to industry must be deliberate, and must aspire to the latest scientific achievements. If we obtain the advanced tools of work, we not only make a sound start, but we also make up for our underdevelopment.

By means of new equipment, Egyptian industry can compensate for the industrial progress which started in other countries at a time when the production instruments were not as advanced as they are now.

We must put aside the fear that modern machines do not need large labour forces. This may be sound in the short term but it is not valid in the long run. For modern machinery enlarges the base of production quickly. This opens new horizons for industrialisation, and so gives wider prospects of employment.

The field for industrial work in Egypt is unlimited. It could extend all over the Egyptian land.

The sources of natural and mineral wealth still keep many of their secrets. Large areas of land have been neglected for long. Efforts aimed hitherto at exploiting them were but scratches on its surface.

Great concern must also be directed to consumer industries. Apart from offering great possibilities of work, those industries meet an important share of consumer demands and save foreign currency. In addition, these industries offer export possibilities. The food industries, in particular, can build up the economy.

Industry has to preserve the essential human equilibrium between development demands and consumer needs, and despite the definite priority that must be given to heavy industry, it must not be allowed to hamper the progress of consumer industries.

The masses of our people have long been deprived; to mobilise them completely for the building of heavy industry and overlook their consumer needs is incompatible with their right to be compensated for their long deprivation.

The position of Labour in the new society was established by the Laws of July 1961 which ensured a minimum wage, positive participation in management coupled with a share in production profit. One result was that the working day has been fixed at seven hours.

This revolutionary change in Labour's rights must be met with a revolutionary change in Labour's duties.

Labour must be responsible for the production equipment placed at its disposal by society.

The new system does not abolish the role of labour organisation, but rather adds to its importance. Labour organisations are no longer a mere counterpart of management in the production operation, but have become the vanguard in development, concerned with safeguarding Labour's rights and interests and with raising the workmen's material and cultural standards. This includes plans for co-operative housing, and co-operative consumption as well as the organisation of sick and convalescence leave.

The maintenance of the private sector alongside the public sector renders control over public ownership more effective. By encouraging competition within the general framework of the economic planning, the private sector is an invigorating element for the public sector.

The July 1961 revolutionary laws were not intended to destroy the private sector. They had two basic aims: The creation of some form of economic entity among the citizens which, while protecting their legitimate rights, would remove the possibility of minority monopolies. The intension was to dissolve class distinctions while preserving the possibilities of peaceful competition and to pave the way for democratic solutions to the problems of development. A further aim was to enable the private to step up the efficiency of the public sector. The door was also left open to private investment in the field of development, at a reasonable dividend.

Those who claim that the July laws restrict private initiative are committing a grave error. Private enterprise should be based on work and risk. In the past, everything was based on opportunism rather than work, and on the protection of monopoly, excluding every possibility of risk.

Private enterprise, as it existed, was incapable of shouldering responsibly the needs of the nation. The new investments now directed towards industry are a hundred times as much as the amount invested in the year preceding the Revolution.

Foreign capital and its investment role is a question we should deal with at this stage. Foreign capital is regarded with suspicion in underdeveloped countries, particularly in those which were formerly colonies.

The sovereignty of the people over their own land and their restoration to the helm, allow them to set conditions under which foreign capital may be invested in their country.

The matter calls for the consideration of their own national needs. It must also take into account the nature of world capital which is to seek unexploited raw materials, often in areas not yet ready for economic or social revival, where the highest profits are obtainable.

In the first place, all foreign aid with no strings attached is acceptable to help attain our national objectives. The aid is accepted with sincere gratitude from those who offer it, regardless of the colour of their flags.

In the second place, all unconditional loans are accepted provided they can be refunded without undue strain.

In the third place, foreign capital is accepted in indispensable operations, especially those requiring new experience, difficult to find in our own country. Acceptance of foreign investment may mean that foreigners would participate in the administration of a project. It may also imply that a share of the annual profits would be payable to the investors indefinitely. Such deals need careful qualifications and safeguards.

Awakened by the revolution to a new conception of history, our people believe the states with a colonialist past are, more than others, under obligation to offer to the nations aspiring to development part of the wealth they tapped when that was there for the taking.

Society is formed of individuals living on the soil of the homeland and bound by their hopes for the future. The true object of economic production is to provide a full and prosperous life for society, and as the base of production expands, new scope is afforded for the whole population.

The concept of social freedom carries with it certain basic rights for every citizen, which we must strive to establish.

First, the right of each citizen to medical care, and then the right to receive education appropriate to his ability and talent. Then there is the right to an adequate job according with ability and education, together with a legally sanctioned minimum wage. And, finally, there is the right to old age benefits.

Woman must be regarded as equal to man and must shed the remaining shackles that impede her from taking a constructive part in life. The family is the primary cell in society, and as such it must be afforded every protection in the national interest.

The freedom of religious belief is a basic right in our new free life.

The spiritual values derived from religions are capable of guiding man, of lighting the candle of faith in his life and of bestowing on him unlimited capacities for integrity and care. In essence, all divine revelation is a human revolution aimed at restoring man's true dignity and happiness. It is the prime duty of religious thinkers, then, to preserve for each religion the essence of its divine message.

The essence of religious revelation does not conflict with our outlook on life. Conflict arises only when attempts are made by reactionary elements to exploit religion—against its nature and spirit—with a view to impeding progress. These elements fabricate interpretations of religion in flagrant contradiction with its real nobility and divine wisdom.

Free conviction is the basis of all faith. Without freedom, faith turns into fanaticism which is a barrier that shuts out all new thought and keeps those who suffer from it untouched by the current of evolution.

Freedom of speech is the first premise of democracy.

The rule of law is its safeguard.

Freedom of speech is the expression of freedom of thought. Safeguards must be provided for freedom of the press, which is the outstanding form of freedom of speech. But like representative councils, the free press should be an honest interpreter and critic of the popular will.

True democracy, in its profoundest sense, eliminates the contradiction between the people and the government, as it transforms the latter into a popular instrument.

The new society, which the Arab people of Egypt are building on the basis of sufficiency and justice for everyone, needs a strong shield in a world where moral standards have not kept pace with intellectual progress.

The role of the United Arab Republic armed forces is to defend the process of social construction against external dangers. The armed forces must be ready to crush any reactionary attempt at preventing the people from fulfilling their great hopes.

Although there is no doubt that self-development is the best way of defence, we must nevertheless realise that we live in an area exposed to aggressive ambitions. The prime aim of our enemies is to prevent us from reaching the strength of full development, so that we may always remain at their mercy.

The United Arab Republic which is in the vanguard of the Arab progressive struggle, is the natural target of all the enemies of the Arab nation and of its progress.

The real danger emanates from the fact that Israel is the tool of imperialism.

At present the United Arab Republic is, both historically and actually the only Arab nation which can assume the responsibility of building a national army, capable of deterring the Zionists' aggressive plans.

8. THE PRACTICAL APPLICATION OF SOCIALISM

Only through creative human action can society realise its aims and ideals. Human effort is the key to progress.

In past centuries other societies have been able to generate their drive and to provide investment for national development, through carrying off the wealth of their colonies.

Other societies exploited the working class to serve the interests of capitalism.

Yet other societies, in their experimental stage, imposed extremely cruel pressure on whole generations, depriving them of the fruit of their labour in the interests of a promised future that they themselves would never see.

The spirit of our times can no longer tolerate all this.

Mankind has now become aware of the evils of imperialism, and has pledged itself to get rid of it.

The working class can no longer be driven, under threat of forced labour, to realise the norms of planned economic systems.

The creative energies of peoples can be inspired to shape the morrow but cannot be driven towards it by bloody enforcement measures.

Scientific progress makes it possible and practical for peoples to find their dynamism without resorting to such obsolete means.

Organised national action based on scientific planning is the path to the desired future.

Every citizen needs to be aware of his responsibility within the overall plan; also of the rights due to him if it is successful.

The philosophy behind national action must reach the workers in every part of the country, and it should reach them in the manner best suited to each.

This is to ensure that thought is constantly linked to reality and theory to practice.

Mental clarity is essential for the success of experiment: as experiment, in its turn, increases clarity of thought, enriches it and relates it to reality.

It is most necessary also to encourage the written word so that it may be a link among all, and give continuity for the future.

Great periods of change are naturally full of dangers. The greatest insurance against these dangers, however, lies in preserving the basic freedoms and enabling them to find expression through elected popular councils.

To apply democracy, the popular councils should have

authority over all production centres and over the machinery of local and central administration. This will guarantee that the objectives of production will remain in the hands of the people.

The exercise of criticism and self-criticism gives an opportunity to correct and adjust national policy to its great objectives.

Freedom for constructive criticism, and courageous self-criticism are a necessary factor, and such freedom will mobilise elements who may otherwise hesitate to participate in the national action, inducing them to work willingly for the objectives of the struggle.

The free discussion which followed the great operation of redistributing the national wealth in July 1961 did not endanger the struggle for change. It was, in fact, a safety-valve for it.

Further, freedom creates new leadership and creates a fund of collective thought capable of checking the arbitrary tendencies of individuals and thus providing a long-term safeguard for national policy. For real leadership involves sensitivity to the demands of the people.

To get the people's energies into action, hopes must not be exaggerated. The real changes will be achieved by looking forward on a long-term basis. And it is most necessary in this period to make it clear that the achievement of the aspired objectives is difficult. The mere changing of the structure of the society of the past does not, in itself, realise the dreams of the masses. Sustained effort alone is capable of converting dreams into realities.

The new leadership undertaking the task of national development has to create an enormous force which must be maintained if it is to be successful. The wealth of experts and technicians which this country possesses is very great and must be vigilantly guarded and developed. But such elements may wrongly assume that the great problems of development can be solved by the complicated procedures of bureaucracy and administration. Such procedures can add fresh burdens to the national effort without necessarily helping it.

If allowed to persevere, these people could become an insulating class that would stop the flow of revolutionary action and prevent its effects from reaching the masses who are in need of them. Administration commits a grievous error if it imagines its machinery to be an end in itself. Such machinery is only a means of service to the people.

The new leadership must be aware of its social role. The gravest danger would be for it to imagine itself to represent a new privileged class replacing the old.

In the process of national development those in charge of great projects need to see that over-expenditure, even when no private profit is involved, is a form of betrayal; it is a squandering of the wealth of the people.

Revolutionary action should be realistic and forward-looking. The revolution is not an action to wipe out the ruins of the past but rather to build up the future.

Science is the weapon of revolutionary purpose. Here emerges the great role to be undertaken by the universities and educational centres on all levels.

The responsibility of the universities and scientific research centres in shaping the future is no less important than that of the various political institutions.

The universities are not ivory towers but rather pace-setters discovering a new way of life for the people.

'Science for society' should be the motto of the cultural revolution at the present stage. The achievement of the objectives of the national struggle will enable us at a further stage of our development, to make our positive contribution to the world in the domain of science.

'Science for society' is not a concept that binds the

scientist to deal with problems of every day life. This would be a limited interpretation.

We should not waste a moment before entering the atomic age. We lagged behind in the age of steam and in the age of electricity. This underdevelopment is costing us a great deal. We are now required, at the dawn of the atomic age, to join those who have embarked upon it.

Atomic energy for war is not our objective.

Atomic energy for prosperity is able to perform miracles in the struggle of national development, just as spiritual energies which people derive from their religious experience and heritage can equally perform miracles.

These spiritual energies can provide a dynamic power for the realisation of great ideals. They also arm people with patience and courage, with which to overcome difficulties and obstacles.

While the organisation of development requires, of necessity, material foundations, spiritual and moral incentives alone are able to inspire this development with the highest ideals and objectives.

9. ARAB UNITY

The United Arab Republic feels a responsibility towards the whole Arab nation.

The Arab nation has a unity of language, forming a unity of mind and thought; it has in common those feelings and aspirations that spring from a common history.

Those who attempt to undermine the concept of Arab unity, quoting the differences among the Arab states, are looking at the matter superficially.

The very existence of those differences underlines the existence of an over-arching unity.

These differences stem largely from the Arab social conflict.

The differences in the objectives of the various Arab rulers reflect the varying stages of development attained.

The course that served an earlier stage of the national struggle, namely that of political revolt against imperialism, has been superseded.

Imperialism has now changed its attitude and has become incapable of directly confronting the people. It now works through the palaces of reaction.

Imperialism, in fact, has unwittingly helped the coming of social revolution by identifying itself with, and making use of, the exploiting elements in certain countries.

Unity cannot be, nor should it be, imposed. The nation's objectives should be equally honourable in their means as in their ends. Therefore, coercion of any kind is detrimental to unity.

Not only is tyranny immoral but it also constitutes a menace to the internal unity of certain Arab people and therefore is a threat to the concept of a united Arab nation.

Arab unity is not a set constitutional formula that must inevitably be applied. It is rather a long path with many stages leading to an ultimate aim.

Any partial unification within the Arab world by two or more of the Arab states is a step forward, drawing nearer the day of total unity.

The United Arab Republic, firmly convinced that it is an integral part of the Arab nation, has a duty to make its call for unity and to stand at the disposal of the Arab people as a whole, not fearing for one minute to be accused of interfering in the affairs of others.

In this sphere, however, the United Arab Republic should take care not to become involved in local party disputes in any Arab state. This would be unworthy of the call for unity.

10. FOREIGN POLICY

The foreign policy of the people of the United Arab Republic is a faithful reflection of their national aims. If the foreign policy of a people ceases to be such a reflection it becomes a sham. It is a farce when certain governments try to mislead by borrowing a glittering foreign policy which does not truly represent the nation's real aspirations.

The foreign policy of the United Arab Republic runs in three lines. The first of these is rejection of attempts to dominate by any outside power; and opposition to such, by every possible means.

Secondly, the pursuit of peace, since conditions of peace are the only hope for the achievement of national progress.

Thirdly, international co-operation, for the prosperity of mankind is no longer divisible and to achieve it, co-operation has now become imperative.

In their fight against imperialism, the people of the U.A.R. have set an example which is still a legend in the history of the struggles of peoples. Our people have stood against three empires, the Ottoman, the French and the British, resisted the invasion of their soil and emerged triumphant in the end.

After decades of foreign domination our people managed to make the forces of aggression evacuate twice in one year. That was in 1956, a decisive year in our national struggle.

The foreigner evacuated our country according to an agreement put into effect in June 1956. He was soon to come back. In October of the same year, thinking that it was able to subjugate the will of our people, to humiliate them and oblige them to submit, he returned.

Our people were determined to protect their independence and to reject all the tricks designed to drag them into spheres of influence. They had led a stupendous resistance in the whole of the Middle East against the Baghdad Pact and now they did not hesitate to oppose the armed tripartite aggression in which two of the world's great powers took part. These powers launched their attack from Israel, the base of imperialism, which was brought into existence with the object of intimidating and splitting the Arab nation.

In the battle of Suez, imperialism revealed itself, its bases and its accomplices.

Armed imperialism pounced upon the people of Egypt because they were trying to realise their independence and achieve progress by making use of one of their own national resources which had for long been exploited by foreigners, and whose value and profits they had monopolised.

By their steadfastness and their resolute fighting against the invaders, the Egyptian people managed to shake the world conscience, and the battle became a turning point in the history of liberation movements.

The bitter defeat of France, Britain and Israel in the Suez War put an end to the age of armed imperialistic adventures. Thanks to the struggle of our people, the end of that loathsome age came for all the peoples of the world. Yet our people remained on the alert, and opposed all military pacts aimed at drawing peoples, against their own will, into the orbit of imperialism.

The insistence of our people on liquidating Israeli aggression is a determination to end one of the most dangerous surviving manifestations of imperialism. Our exposure of the Israeli policy of infiltration in Africa is only an attempt to limit the spread of a destructive imperialist cancer.

The insistence of our people on resisting racial discrimination expresses a clear understanding of its real significance. Racial discrimination is only a method of exploiting the wealth and efforts of peoples. Discrimination between people on the basis of colour paves the way for a discrimination between the value of their efforts.

Our people have spared no effort in their pursuit of peace; and the sincerity of their call for peace arises from their dire need for it. Without peace they are unable to pursue their struggle for development, and it is this realisation that has led them to adopt a policy of non-alignment and positive neutrality in foreign affairs.

International co-operation for prosperity is the ultimate foreign policy aim of the U.A.R., which is a logical development of the national struggle. Our people offer their hand to all peoples and nations working for international peace and human prosperity. We believe that prosperity is indivisible, and that international co-operation for prosperity could become the strongest guarantee of international peace.

The clash that could break out between developed and underdeveloped countries is the second danger that threatens international peace. The first is the possibility of a surprise nuclear war.

International co-operation for prosperity, which would narrow the gap between the standards of nations and sow the seeds of love between them, instead of the seeds of hatred, offers a hope.

International co-operation for prosperity on the part of the developed countries would be a way of restitution for the age of imperialism, a restitution made by those responsible for that age as well as by many who were not.

International co-operation covers a wide field, in which the U.A.R. tries to play its part. It includes the sharing of scientific secrets because a monopoly of science could threaten humanity. It also includes the peaceful use of atomic energy, in the service of development.

Again, it must envisage the transference of huge funds spent on the manufacture of nuclear weapons to the service of life instead of the opposite.

While our people believe in Arab unity, they also believe in a pan-African movement and in Afro-Asian solidarity. They believe in the close spiritual bond that ties them to the Islamic world. They believe in the U.N., and are loyal to the U.N. Charter, which is the outcome of the suffering of peoples in two world wars.

There is no contradiction between these ideals. In fact they form links of one chain.

Our people live at the north-eastern gate of struggling Africa and cannot be isolated from its political, social and economic development.

Our people belong to the two continents, where the greatest battles of national liberation rage. These battles are an outstanding feature of the twentieth century.

Our people believe in the messages of religion, and they live in the area where those divine messages were first received. They are determined to reform the way of life in their own land, by pursuing freedom, truth, efficiency, justice, love and peace.

Our people have a strong enough faith in God and in themselves to enable them to get to grips with life, and to re-model it according to their highest hopes and ideals.

Index

INDEX